S0-CTN-308

MEMORY
AND
LEARNING

THE ENCYCLOPEDIA OF
H E A L T H

THE HEALTHY BODY

Dale C. Garell, M.D. · General Editor

MEMORY
AND
LEARNING

Nancy Wartik and
LaVonne Carlson-Finnerty

Introduction by C. Everett Koop, M.D., Sc.D.

former Surgeon General, U. S. Public Health Service

CHELSEA HOUSE PUBLISHERS

New York · Philadelphia

The goal of the ENCYCLOPEDIA OF HEALTH *is to provide general information in the ever-changing areas of physiology, psychology, and related medical issues. The titles in this series are not intended to take the place of the professional advice of a physician or other health care professional.*

CHELSEA HOUSE PUBLISHERS
EDITOR-IN-CHIEF   Richard S. Papale
EXECUTIVE MANAGING EDITOR   Karyn Gullen Browne
COPY CHIEF   Philip Koslow
PICTURE EDITOR   Adrian G. Allen
ART DIRECTOR   Nora Wertz
MANUFACTURING DIRECTOR   Gerald Levine
SYSTEMS MANAGER   Lindsey Ottman
PRODUCTION COORDINATOR   Marie Claire Cebrián-Ume

The Encyclopedia of Health
SENIOR EDITOR   Kenneth W. Lane

Staff for MEMORY AND LEARNING
COPY EDITOR   David Carter
EDITORIAL ASSISTANT   Laura Petermann
PICTURE RESEARCHER   Sandy Jones
DESIGNER   Robert Yaffe

First Printing
1   3   5   7   9   8   6   4   2

Library of Congress Cataloging-in-Publication Data

Carlson-Finnerty, LaVonne.
    Memory and learning/by LaVonne Carlson-Finnerty and Nancy Wartik; introduction
by C. Everett Koop.
        p. cm. —(The Encyclopedia of health)
    Includes bibliographical references and index.
    Summary: An examination of the memory and learning processes, the functioning of
the brain, and memory and learning disorders.
    ISBN 0-7910-0022-2
        0-7910-0462-7 (pbk.)
    1. Memory—Juvenile literature. 2. Learning, Psychology of—Juvenile literature. [1.
Memory. 2. Learning—Psychology.] I. Wartik, Nancy. II. Title. III. Series.
BF375.C37 1992   92-10544
153.1—dc20   CIP
                                                                                       AC

CONTENTS

THE ENCYCLOPEDIA OF
H E A L T H

PREVENTION AND EDUCATION: THE KEYS TO GOOD HEALTH

C. Everett Koop, M.D., Sc.D.
former Surgeon General,
U.S. Public Health Service

The issue of health education has received particular attention in recent years because of the presence of AIDS in the news. But our response to this particular tragedy points up a number of broader issues that doctors, public health officials, educators, and the public face. In particular, it points up the necessity for sound health education for citizens of all ages.

Over the past 25 years this country has been able to bring about dramatic declines in the death rates for heart disease, stroke, accidents, and for people under the age of 45, cancer. Today, Americans generally eat better and take better care of themselves than ever before. Thus, with the help of modern science and technology, they have a better chance of surviving serious—even catastrophic—illnesses. That's the good news.

But, like every phonograph record, there's a flip side, and one with special significance for young adults. According to a report issued in 1979 by Dr. Julius Richmond, my predecessor as Surgeon General, Americans aged 15 to 24 had a higher death rate in 1979 than they did 20 years earlier. The causes: violent death and injury, alcohol and drug abuse, unwanted pregnancies, and sexually transmitted diseases. Adolescents are particularly vulnerable because they are beginning to explore their own sexuality and perhaps to experiment with drugs. The need for educating young people is critical, and the price of neglect is high.

Yet even for the population as a whole, our health is still far from what it could be. Why? A 1974 Canadian government report attributed all death and disease to four broad elements: inadequacies in the health care system, behavioral factors or unhealthy life-styles, environmental hazards, and human biological factors.

To be sure, there are diseases that are still beyond the control of even our advanced medical knowledge and techniques. And despite yearnings that are as old as the human race itself, there is no "fountain of youth" to ward off aging and death. Still, there is a solution to many of the problems that undermine sound health. In a word, that solution is prevention. Prevention, which includes health promotion and education, saves lives, improves the quality of life, and in the long run, saves money.

In the United States, organized public health activities and preventive medicine have a long history. Important milestones in this country or foreign breakthroughs adopted in the United States include the improvement of sanitary procedures and the development of pasteurized milk in the late 19th century and the introduction in the mid-20th century of effective vaccines against polio, measles, German measles, mumps, and other once-rampant diseases. Internationally, organized public health efforts began on a wide-scale basis with the International Sanitary Conference of 1851, to which 12 nations sent representatives. The World Health Organization, founded in 1948, continues these efforts under the aegis of the United Nations, with particular emphasis on combating communicable diseases and the training of health care workers.

Despite these accomplishments, much remains to be done in the field of prevention. For too long, we have had a medical care system that is science- and technology-based, focused, essentially, on illness and mortality. It is now patently obvious that both the social and the economic costs of such a system are becoming insupportable.

Implementing prevention—and its corollaries, health education and promotion—is the job of several groups of people.

First, the medical and scientific professions need to continue basic scientific research, and here we are making considerable progress. But increased concern with prevention will also have a decided impact on how primary care doctors practice medicine. With a shift to health-based rather than morbidity-based medicine, the role of the "new physician" will include a healthy dose of patient education.

Second, practitioners of the social and behavioral sciences—psychologists, economists, city planners—along with lawyers, business leaders, and government officials—must solve the practical and ethical dilemmas confronting us: poverty, crime, civil rights, literacy, education, employment, housing, sanitation, environmental protection, health care delivery systems, and so forth. All of these issues affect public health.

Third is the public at large. We'll consider that very important group in a moment.

8

Fourth, and the linchpin in this effort, is the public health profession—doctors, epidemiologists, teachers—who must harness the professional expertise of the first two groups and the common sense and cooperation of the third, the public. They must define the problems statistically and qualitatively and then help us set priorities for finding the solutions.

To a very large extent, improving those statistics is the responsibility of every individual. So let's consider more specifically what the role of the individual should be and why health education is so important to that role. First, and most obvious, individuals can protect themselves from illness and injury and thus minimize their need for professional medical care. They can eat nutritious food; get adequate exercise; avoid tobacco, alcohol, and drugs; and take prudent steps to avoid accidents. The proverbial "apple a day keeps the doctor away" is not so far from the truth, after all.

Second, individuals should actively participate in their own medical care. They should schedule regular medical and dental checkups. Should they develop an illness or injury, they should know when to treat themselves and when to seek professional help. To gain the maximum benefit from any medical treatment that they do require, individuals must become partners in that treatment. For instance, they should understand the effects and side effects of medications. I counsel young physicians that there is no such thing as too much information when talking with patients. But the corollary is the patient must know enough about the nuts and bolts of the healing process to understand what the doctor is telling him or her. That is at least partially the patient's responsibility.

Education is equally necessary for us to understand the ethical and public policy issues in health care today. Sometimes individuals will encounter these issues in making decisions about their own treatment or that of family members. Other citizens may encounter them as jurors in medical malpractice cases. But we all become involved, indirectly, when we elect our public officials, from school board members to the president. Should surrogate parenting be legal? To what extent is drug testing desirable, legal, or necessary? Should there be public funding for family planning, hospitals, various types of medical research, and other medical care for the indigent? How should we allocate scant technological resources, such as kidney dialysis and organ transplants? What is the proper role of government in protecting the rights of patients?

What are the broad goals of public health in the United States today? In 1980, the Public Health Service issued a report aptly entitled *Promoting Health—Preventing Disease: Objectives for the Nation*. This report expressed its goals in terms of mortality and in terms of intermediate goals in education and health improvement. It identified 15 major concerns: controlling high blood pressure; improving family planning; improving pregnancy care and infant health; increasing the rate of immunization; controlling sexually transmitted diseases; controlling the presence of toxic agents and radiation in the environment; improving occupational safety and health; preventing accidents; promoting water fluoridation and dental health; controlling infectious diseases; decreasing smoking; decreasing alcohol and drug abuse; improving nutrition; promoting physical fitness and exercise; and controlling stress and violent behavior.

For healthy adolescents and young adults (ages 15 to 24), the specific goal was a 20% reduction in deaths, with a special focus on motor vehicle injuries and alcohol and drug abuse. For adults (ages 25 to 64), the aim was 25% fewer deaths, with a concentration on heart attacks, strokes, and cancers.

Smoking is perhaps the best example of how individual behavior can have a direct impact on health. Today, cigarette smoking is recognized as the single most important preventable cause of death in our society. It is responsible for more cancers and more cancer deaths than any other known agent; is a prime risk factor for heart and blood vessel disease, chronic bronchitis, and emphysema; and is a frequent cause of complications in pregnancies and of babies born prematurely, underweight, or with potentially fatal respiratory and cardiovascular problems.

Since the release of the Surgeon General's first report on smoking in 1964, the proportion of adult smokers has declined substantially, from 43% in 1965 to 30.5% in 1985. Since 1965, 37 million people have quit smoking. Although there is still much work to be done if we are to become a "smoke-free society," it is heartening to note that public health and public education efforts—such as warnings on cigarette packages and bans on broadcast advertising—have already had significant effects.

In 1835, Alexis de Tocqueville, a French visitor to America, wrote, "In America the passion for physical well-being is general." Today, as then, health and fitness are front-page items. But with the greater scientific and technological resources now available to us, we are in a far stronger position to make good health care available to everyone. And with the greater technological threats to us as we approach the 21st century, the need to do so is more urgent than ever before. Comprehensive information about basic biology, preventive medicine, medical and surgical treatments, and related ethical and public policy issues can help you arm yourself with the knowledge you need to be healthy throughout your life.

FOREWORD

Dale C. Garell, M.D.

Advances in our understanding of health and disease during the 20th century have been truly remarkable. Indeed, it could be argued that modern health care is one of the greatest accomplishments in all of human history. In the early 20th century, improvements in sanitation, water treatment, and sewage disposal reduced death rates and increased longevity. Previously untreatable illnesses can now be managed with antibiotics, immunizations, and modern surgical techniques. Discoveries in the fields of immunology, genetic diagnosis, and organ transplantation are revolutionizing the prevention and treatment of disease. Modern medicine is even making inroads against cancer and heart disease, two of the leading causes of death in the United States.

Although there is much to be proud of, medicine continues to face enormous challenges. Science has vanquished diseases such as smallpox and polio, but new killers, most notably AIDS, confront us. Moreover, we now victimize ourselves with what some have called "diseases of choice," or those brought on by drug and alcohol abuse, bad eating habits, and mismanagement of the stresses and strains of contemporary life. The very technology that is doing so much to prolong life has brought with it previously unimaginable ethical dilemmas related to issues of death and dying. The rising cost of health care is a matter of central concern to us all. And violence in the form of automobile accidents, homicide, and suicide remains the major killer of young adults.

In the past, most people were content to leave health care and medical treatment in the hands of professionals. But since the 1960s, the consumer of medical care—that is, the patient—has assumed an increasingly central role in the management of his or her own health. There has also been a new emphasis placed on prevention: People are recognizing that their own actions can help prevent many of the conditions that have caused death and disease in the past. This accounts for the growing commitment to good nutrition and regular exercise, for the increasing number of people who are choosing not to smoke, and for a new moderation in people's drinking habits.

People want to know more about themselves and their own health. They are curious about their body: its anatomy, physiology, and biochemistry. They want to keep up with rapidly evolving medical technologies and procedures. They are willing to educate themselves about common disorders and diseases so that they can be full partners in their own health care.

THE ENCYCLOPEDIA OF HEALTH is designed to provide the basic knowledge that readers will need if they are to take significant responsibility for their own health. It is also meant to serve as a frame of reference for further study and exploration. The encyclopedia is divided into five subsections: The Healthy Body; The Life Cycle; Medical Disorders & Their Treatment; Psychological Disorders & Their Treatment; and Medical Issues. For each topic covered by the encyclopedia, we present the essential facts about the relevant biology; the symptoms, diagnosis, and treatment of common diseases and disorders; and ways in which you can prevent or reduce the severity of health problems when that is possible. The encyclopedia also projects what may lie ahead in the way of future treatment or prevention strategies.

The broad range of topics and issues covered in the encyclopedia reflects that human health encompasses physical, psychological, social, environmental, and spiritual well-being. Just as the mind and the body are inextricably linked, so, too, is the individual an integral part of the wider world that comprises his or her family, society, and environment. To discuss health in its broadest aspect it is necessary to explore the many ways in which it is connected to such fields as law, social science, public policy, economics, and even religion. And so, the encyclopedia is meant to be a bridge between science, medical technology, the world at large, and you. I hope that it will inspire you to pursue in greater depth particular areas of interest and that you will take advantage of the suggestions for further reading and the lists of resources and organizations that can provide additional information.

CHAPTER 1

EARLY THEORIES AND RESEARCH

Memory and learning are not merely tools to be used at school and in the workplace for the purpose of absorbing facts, generating ideas, and acquiring new skills, but are lifelong processes vital to the development of an individual's sense of identity.

"Live and learn!" is an old saying that people generally use after making a mistake. But people gain knowledge not only from wrong actions. They constantly absorb facts, generate ideas, undergo new experiences, and develop new impressions. With the information thus gained, they can reach understandings and make decisions.

Many people tend to think of memory and learning as tools to be used in school. They view learning as the acquisition of new facts, such as historic dates or mathematic formulas. Memory seems most useful at examination time. In fact, people rely on their capacity to learn and remember even after school is long over.

The 19th-century Irish writer Oscar Wilde called memory "the diary that we all carry around with us." Without this mental record of the past—of the people, places, and events that shape a life—a person would lack a sense of identity. With no ability to recognize familiar surroundings or faces, people would walk through life as strangers even to themselves.

DEFINING MEMORY AND LEARNING

Because memory and learning do not operate independently of each other, they are not easy to distinguish. In everyday speech, the two words are often used interchangeably. Someone may say "I *memorized* the lyrics of 'The Star-Spangled Banner'" and mean "I *learned* the lyrics . . ."

Learning is the active process of gaining a skill or knowledge. It implies understanding of how to perform an action such as baking a cake, riding a bicycle, or solving a mathematics problem. Memory involves the mental storage and locating process—the retaining and recalling of what has been learned. Thus, learning depends on memory.

To define memory and learning more precisely is difficult. There are many types of memory and many methods of learning. Learning can be described as "a relatively permanent change in behavior that occurs because of experience or practice." For instance, a child who burns his hand on a hot stove learns not to touch hot stoves, and a young woman who breaks her training schedule and fails tryouts for the track team learns that she will have to train regularly if she wants to make next year's team.

IN ANCIENT DAYS

Today, people who make speeches or who have to present large amounts of information to an audience, such as politicians, lawyers, teachers, and television newscasters, can refer to written notes or a

TelePrompTer. But writing materials were a luxury in Greek and Roman times. Printing presses, computers, and video and audio equipment did not exist. Often, people relied entirely on memory to record the past.

A Memory Device

Around 500 or 600 B.C., the Greeks developed a special system to aid memory. They discovered that data are best recalled when associated with familiar objects placed in an orderly fashion in the mind's eye. Envisioning a structure like a house—usually one with many rooms, nooks, and crannies—they mentally walked through and memorized a certain sequence of areas. In each area they imagined pictures that would recall an idea. They could then mentally walk through the house seeing a sequence of images that recalled an entire speech, poem, or story.

If, for example, the Greeks' system of aiding memory was to be applied to the Reverend Martin Luther King's famous civil rights speech of August 28, 1963, in Washington, D.C., it might have begun by envisioning a spacious marble building. In one part of his speech, King said, "I have a dream that one day on the red hills of Georgia, sons of former slaves and sons of former slave-owners will be able to sit down together at the table of brotherhood." Under the Greek system of associating dreaming with sleep, the front hall of the building might have held a man asleep, as a preamble to further concepts embodied in King's speech. Each of these concepts would then be housed within the building and arranged in different rooms in the order in which they occur in the speech. One room might therefore hold a painting of red hills, another of children gathered together and eating, and so forth.

This memory system may seem complicated, and perhaps not everyone could train themselves to use it. But some Greeks and Romans learned to use the "memory house"—or in its Greek derivation *mnemonic*—technique very effectively. A Roman teacher named Seneca was known for having repeated 2,000 names in order, after hearing them just once.

Principles of Memory and Learning

In sharpening their memory for practical use, the Greeks and Romans uncovered a number of principles of memory and learning that still hold true today. A 1st-century B.C. Roman observation—clearly as true today as it was then—was that the mind often retains things that are "exceptionally . . . unusual, great, unbelievable, or ridiculous" more easily than those that are commonplace. Thus, in order to improve recall, the Greeks and Romans used the oddest images they could find in their memory houses.

Ancient philosophers often speculated on the nature of memory and learning. The 4th-century B.C. Greek philosopher Plato suggested that memory could be understood by imagining that "our minds contain a block of wax." Into this block, he theorized, the thoughts and experiences that form memories are inscribed in much the same way that a stick might inscribe words in clay.

His view of the learning process was that the mind of a newborn was like a giant birdcage that gradually fills with different kinds of

A woodcut of Aristotle (384–322 B.C.) and his pupil Alexander. Some of the earliest theories of memory and learning are still current. For more than 2,000 years, philosophers and scientists have drawn upon Aristotle's analysis of how the mind recalls the past through association.

birds. In this metaphor for learning, Plato supposed that "the birds are kinds of knowledge, and that when we were children, this [cage] was empty."

Aristotle, a renowned student of Plato, discussed another important aspect of memory, *association*. This process occurs when someone mentally connects separate perceptions or ideas in a way that makes them meaningful. Thus, thinking of one thing calls the other to mind. A series of mental jumps from one idea to another—a "train of thought"—is one form of association. Remembering to turn off the oven upon hearing the ring of the timer is another.

Aristotle believed that people recall the past by using association in one of three ways: through thoughts that are similar (thinking about a lake brings the ocean to mind); thoughts that are opposite (hot calls cold to mind); or thoughts that are closely connected in time or place (Christmas falls close to New Year's Day). Simple as it sounds, Aristotle's analysis remains one of the most influential ideas about how the mind works. Over the past 2,000 years, other thinkers have used his work as a basis to develop their own theories on how the processes of memory and learning operate.

THE SCIENTIFIC APPROACH

By the end of the 19th century, theories on memory and learning were plentiful, but there was little data to support them. Scientists did not see how these complex, invisible processes could be measured or studied in experiments, and therefore left the matter to the attention of philosophers.

Ebbinghaus Measures Memory

In 1879, a 29-year-old German psychologist named Hermann Ebbinghaus decided it was possible to do more than theorize about memory. Using himself as the subject in a series of experiments, he set out to answer specific questions about how written material is learned and recalled.

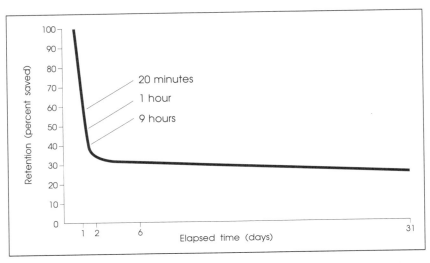

In the late 19th century, Hermann Ebbinghaus proved that the scientific method could be used to analyze memory and learning. His forgetting curve showed how time affects memory: forgetting is at first rapid and extensive but eventually levels off, after which the mind can recall a portion of the information originally learned.

Ebbinghaus created 2,300 three-letter nonsense syllables, such as ZOD, VIR, and FUD, to memorize. He felt that because real words might be easier to recall, they might therefore distort his results. Day after day, over a period of five years, Ebbinghaus patiently sat memorizing his lists of nonsense syllables by reading them aloud. He timed himself and considered a list as being memorized when he could recite it perfectly on one occasion.

Ebbinghaus found that *overlearning* helps recall. In some cases, after reaching the point at which he had memorized a list, Ebbinghaus read it over 64 extra times. This overlearning, he noted, helped him memorize the same list again the next day with two-thirds fewer readings than the day before.

The young psychologist invented several clever ways to chart how his mind performed during and after this process. In one experiment, Ebbinghaus devised a graph called the *forgetting curve* to show mathematically how time affects recall. Twenty minutes after memorizing a series of lists, he tested himself and found that he had forgotten over

40% of his material. Nine hours later, he had lost 64%. After this, his forgetting leveled off, so that 2 days later he had forgotten 72% of the list, and a month later, 79%.

Ebbinghaus showed that mathematical and scientific methods can be used to measure mental processes, opening new paths in the exploration of memory and learning. Researchers still use some of Ebbinghaus's methods, such as testing memory with nonsense words, and many of his discoveries remain valid today.

Pavlov and Conditioning

About 20 years after Ebbinghaus's experiments, a Russian scientist made another eventful discovery. Ivan Pavlov was investigating the digestion process in dogs. Like a human being, a dog will salivate if it sees or smells food. Pavlov noticed that those dogs that knew the routine in his laboratory began to salivate merely at the sight of an experimenter. The dogs associated being fed with the person's approach.

Pavlov decided to see what this might mean and created an experiment that involved sounding a bell just before the dogs were fed. After a while the dogs knew that the ring of the bell meant "food" and

In the early 20th century, Russian scientist Ivan Pavlov investigated a form of associative learning that occurs through conditioning. Pavlov taught laboratory dogs to associate the sound of a bell with mealtime, so that they would respond to the toll by salivating—a natural reflex usually reserved for food.

salivated at the sound. To salivate over food is a physical *reflex*, an automatic, uncontrollable response. But salivating at the sound of a bell is not a natural reflex; it is a response that occurs because of learning. The dogs in Pavlov's laboratory mentally linked the sound of a bell with food, after closely relating the two in time. For Pavlov, watching this transfer was like seeing the learning process as it happened.

Pavlov described this process of teaching dogs to make a mental association as *conditioning*. Salivating to the sound of a bell, which Pavlov called the *stimulus*, was a *conditioned response*. Such responses represent a form of learning that is prevalent in both animals and humans.

For the rest of his life, Pavlov investigated the "rules" of this sort of associative learning—inquiring into when, how, and under what conditions it happens. Pavlov's accidental finding was the basis for one of the world's most renowned experiments. Today, the term Pavlovian is commonly used to describe an automatic response to something.

Thorndike and Puzzle Boxes

The beginning of the 20th century was a fruitful time for memory and learning research. In New York City, Edward Lee Thorndike, a 24-year-old psychology graduate student at Columbia University, was experimenting in this field with the help of cats.

For his experiments, Thorndike invented *puzzle boxes*, small wooden cages with a door that could be opened from the inside by pulling a string. Inside each box Thorndike put a cat, and outside the box he placed food. Then he watched the cats scratch around, trying to get to the food. Eventually, a cat would accidentally pull the string and release itself from the cage. After a few such accidents, the cats learned what they had to do to escape from the cage.

Thorndike's cats went a step beyond Pavlov's dogs in the learning process. Instead of simply reacting to an outside stimulus, they performed an action to obtain what they wanted. Thorndike's work put a new focus on learning as an active process of trial and error. It also emphasized the importance of *reward* (in this case, food) as a *motivation* for learning.

American psychologist Edward Lee Thorndike studied the importance of motivation to the learning process. The ideas he derived from his experiments with cats changed teaching methods in the American school system.

Thorndike eventually transferred his interest in animal learning to human learning and became a well-known educational psychologist. However, his ideas, which changed teaching methods in the American school system, were influenced by his animal studies. He advised teachers to keep principles of association, repetition, and the need for motivation in mind as they worked with pupils.

Freud and the Subconscious

While Thorndike studied cats in New York, another original thinker, across the Atlantic Ocean in Vienna, Austria, pondered the mysteries of the human *psyche*—an individual's psychological make-up. Sigmund Freud began his career as a medical doctor, but grew more interested in the workings of the mind than the body. His psychological analyses of patients convinced him of the power of the *subconscious*, a part of the mind with ideas, feelings, and memories below the surface of normal awareness.

Freud felt that the subconscious strongly influences a person's personality and behavior. He was particularly interested in how someone's subconscious memories of childhood affect that person's adult personality. Freud's ideas on the subconscious revolutionized 20th-century thought. Though some of his theories are now outdated, almost any discussion of mental processes, including memory and learning, presumes the operation of subconscious processes in ruling human actions.

Conditioned Emotions

In 1919, two psychologists at Johns Hopkins University decided to conduct a unique learning experiment. John Watson and Rosalie Rayner wanted to see if the kind of conditioning that Pavlov had used on dogs would also operate on human emotions. Their subject was a healthy baby boy named Albert.

Watson and Rayner began by observing that nothing frightened Albert except loud noises. They then put a tame white rat near Albert, who reached for it curiously. As he did so, the scientists struck a hammer on a steel bar that made a startling clang. Albert jumped and trembled.

Watson and Rayner repeated this experiment a second time. Again, as the child reached for the rat, they struck the hammer on the bar, and Albert began to cry. Over the next week, they conducted tests in which the sight of the rat was followed by a fearful clang. Soon, Albert cried whenever he saw the rat. He also showed fear of other fuzzy things, such as cotton balls and a fur coat. The psychologists had conditioned Albert to fear the rat and similar objects by leading him to associate them with the frightening noise.

After the experiment ended, Watson and Rayner lost track of Albert, who vanished from history. Today, he would be about 70 years of age. If rats or furry objects still make him nervous, he probably does not know why. Despite the experiment's questionable ethics, which would not meet today's research standards, it was among the first to show that conditioning principles used on animals can also be applied to humans.

Yet conditioning has proven to be only one way in which learning occurs. Humans have developed many techniques to help them adapt to changes in their environments. This adaptation is the basis of learning, a process that will be examined in the next chapter.

CHAPTER 2

TYPES OF LEARNING

Humans are highly adaptable to a variety of habitats. In part, this capacity to adapt to change is possible because of uniquely human ways of learning.

The human species, unlike any other, can live in habitats as varied as the freezing Arctic tundra and the blistering Sahara Desert. Human beings have learned what tools or skills they need to live in these environments and have adjusted accordingly. Throughout human history, the ability to profit by experience and adapt to new circumstances has often been a matter of life or death, for individuals as well as cultures.

Learning has been defined as a relatively permanent change in behavior, occurring because of experience or practice. At a basic level, learning serves the very practical purpose of survival. But learning not to touch a hot stove differs somewhat from learning to read or solve mathematics problems.

LEARNING BY EXPERIENCE

The levels of learning range from the most simple, possessed by all animals, to the most complex, known only in humans. These range from *habituation*—a primitive form of learning—to *concept learning*, one of the most advanced forms. Being able to learn in complex ways is not a substitute for simpler forms of learning. Scientists stress that different types of learning have common roots: association, for instance, plays a part in complex as well as in simple types of learning.

To better understand what learning is, scientists have had to define what it is not. Some of the behavioral changes that occur as a human being or animal matures are not considered learning. Thus, a puppy walks when it is ready to do so, as a result of the maturation of its nervous system, muscles, and bone structure, and without being taught. Learning is different from behavioral changes that result from such biologic development. Likewise, the salivary gland's *reflex*, or automatic response, to food is not a learned behavior. Often, behaviors are inborn methods of protecting the body or keeping it healthy.

Thus, *instinct*, an inborn natural reflex, does not represent learning. Birds migrate when the seasons change, not because they have studied maps or watched a weather report but because instinct drives them to do so. Instinct guides spiders in building webs and squirrels in burying nuts.

Often, biological urges and learning combine to change an individual's behavior, making it hard to separate where one process ends and the other begins. Yet the contribution of each is separate. Children cannot talk before they reach a certain age, and when ready they must learn how to use language properly. The process is not automatic.

Some responses are not learned but are instinctive. Acting on an inborn instinct, birds migrate when the seasons change.

Habituation

The simplest type of learning is *habituation*. This occurs when an animal or human being becomes so used to something in its surroundings that ignoring that thing becomes a habit. Habituation is basically learning *not* to respond to a stimulus. Studies show that when touched, single-celled protozoan organisms—which are among the simplest living creatures—automatically withdraw, but that such withdrawal tends to lessen with repeated touching, as if the protozoan had come to realize that the touch was not a threat.

Other, more complex organisms also demonstrate habituation. A cat may fear the vacuum cleaner and at first run away whenever it is in use. Slowly, however, the cat may discover that even though the machine is noisy, it is harmless. Eventually, the cat habituates, paying no attention as the vacuum cleaner roars by.

Humans also demonstrate habituation. A young man who sees a horror movie featuring a knife-wielding killer may cover his eyes when the violence begins. But halfway through the movie he may start taking peeks. The next time, he may watch a horror movie without covering his face. At a third such movie he may even find the violence boring. He has become habituated to it.

Conditioning

Conditioning, a step up the ladder from habituation, involves making an association between previously unconnected events or things. Pavlov's dogs and baby Albert were conditioned in one way, Thorndike's cats in another. In both cases, outside events combine with mental processes to shape the subject's behavior. If this behavior had been caused by inborn, internal drives, it would be considered an instinctual response.

The first kind of conditioning, often called *classical conditioning*, is based on a reflexive response to an outside stimulus. This response can then be transferred to a second stimulus. The transfer happens automatically because the two stimuli are closely associated in time or place: a rat makes a baby cry because the rat is accompanied by a loud noise.

The second kind of conditioning, *operant conditioning*, involves more than automatic responses. It requires an action that accomplishes a goal or gains a reward: whenever the action is rewarded, a stronger association grows between that action and the desired outcome. Whenever Thorndike's cats accidentally performed the action that gained them the food, the connection between that action and the reward was strengthened. Slowly, the cats' moves became deliberate. If a normally poor student studies hard for a test and does well, he or she may study hard to get a good grade on the next test.

For a half century after Pavlov's and Thorndike's research, scientists studied conditioning intensely. Many new principles about this type of learning emerged. It was discovered, for instance, that conditioning also occurs through *punishment* —unpleasant consequences that follow unwanted behavior. But punishment is only effective when delivered properly. To punish a human being or an animal without showing them another way to behave may be useless. If a cat likes to scratch the sofa, the best way to stop this behavior might be to get a scratching post and reward the cat with food when it uses the post. Simply smacking the cat for scratching the sofa will not help change its behavior.

Skinner's Conditioning

B. F. Skinner, a renowned American psychologist, spent years studying animal conditioning. He invented a special device called the *Skinner box*, which became a widely used research tool. The box is a small cage with a lever or similar mechanism that an animal—usually a rat or pigeon—can learn to press or peck to get food. It differs from

In studying the extent to which an animal can learn through conditioning, B. F. Skinner taught pigeons to play Ping-Pong by motivating them with food.

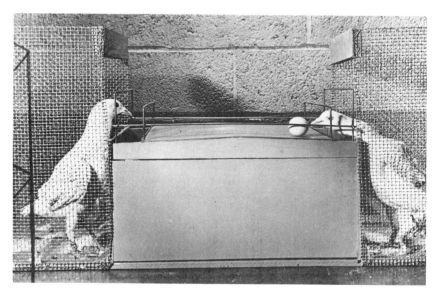

Thorndike's puzzle box because researchers can vary the conditions under which the food is given and can observe how varying these conditions affects learning.

By rewarding a specific kind of behavior, Skinner found that he could greatly expand an animal's ability to learn: he even taught pigeons to play Ping-Pong. He motivated them to peck a ball by giving them a food pellet for each accidental move they made toward the ball, such as looking at it, walking up to it, or touching it. Then he set up a small table, with a pigeon at each end. The birds pecked a ball back and forth across the table until one missed and the ball fell, triggering a food dispenser on the "winning" bird's side of the table. Each bird thus had an incentive to keep the other from returning the serve.

Skinner concluded that rewards increase learning and then applied his theory about animal learning directly to humans. Skinner came to believe that all human behavior results from learned experiences. The learning is based on whether a given action is in some way rewarded, making it more likely to recur. To Skinner, personality, moral values, and feelings are really the sum of how human beings are conditioned in the giant laboratory that is the world. According to this theory, persons who are shy and quiet have either had negative social experiences or have obtained rewards or positive responses when they say less.

Although the principles of conditioning as a source of behavior remain important, few scientists any longer consider them the sole means of learning. Today, many experts instead feel that genetics plays a strong role in determining personality traits. Furthermore, learning has proved a more complex matter than simply forming associations or responding to rewards or punishments.

COGNITIVE LEARNING

Cognitive learning, in which internal mental processes such as thinking are used to change behavior, is currently of intense interest to scientists. Unlike conditioning (which depends on external events), cognitive learning is not always reflected directly in behavior. As a result, it is more difficult to study. However, an ingenious experiment performed in 1930 by the American psychologist Edward Tolman showed that learning occurs in ways that cannot be fully explained by theories on conditioning.

Motivation

Tolman did most of his studies with rats, eventually dedicating a book to these helpful laboratory subjects. In a famous experiment, Tolman ran different groups of rats through a maze. Rats in the first group were rewarded with food for running the maze. Those in the second group were not rewarded. After 10 days, the second group made significantly more mistakes than the first when running the maze. Then Tolman took the rats in the second group and began rewarding them for finishing the maze. They soon found their way with as few errors as the first group.

The results suggested that the rats in the second group had been learning the layout of the maze as they wandered through it. Yet evidence of their learning did not appear until they were offered a reason to perform. Thus, Tolman proved that a reward is not the sole basis for learning; motivation is crucial to performance but does not affect learning ability. Nevertheless, learning may not occur without the proper motivation—the need or desire that prompts activity.

In other work, Tolman showed that rats seem to learn how to travel through a maze in a more complex way than by merely associating a given path with a food reward. When they find a familiar path blocked, they quickly take another one. Apparently, with repeated attempts to find their way through the maze, the rats create a kind of "mental map" of the maze, so that an overall view of it is stored in their brains. Similarly, cognitive maps help humans to maneuver flexibly through the world rather than merely responding to it by habit.

Tolman's work was ahead of its time. Interest in cognitive learning did not become widespread until the 1960s. But psychologists now believe that humans and animals learn by a variety of cognitive methods.

Observational Learning

Observational learning occurs by watching or listening to others speak, act, or respond, and remembering and imitating their behavior when appropriate. Acquiring a skill often depends on this type of learning: driving an automobile, dancing, or playing the guitar without first seeing someone else do these things would be difficult.

Animals also learn by observation. Young songbirds do not automatically begin chirping out their tunes at an early age. To some degree they learn their specific chirping signals by imitating older birds. They

Humans as well as other animals learn by watching others. Young children often learn by imitating what they see their parents do.

even learn to sing with the "accent" of their geographic region, with the result that a single species of bird may produce different sounds in one part of the country than another. Birds that grow up without hearing older birds sing will chirp tunes that are much less varied and complex than those of normal birds.

Young children are great observational learners and often imitate what they see their parents do by playing at cooking, driving cars, or caring for babies. When teaching a child, parents often discover that the things they say are not as important as the things they do, which sometimes have harsh consequences. Children who are hit or beaten by their parents, for example, are six times more likely, when they grow up, to hit their own children. As abused children, they learned by observation that hitting is a valid way to express anger.

Advertisers also make use of a form of learning by observation. By portraying the users of a particular product as sophisticated, good-looking people, whom they assume consumers want to be like, the advertisers hope to induce consumers to want to use the product as well.

Insight

Most people have had the experience of being unable to solve a frustrating problem and then suddenly grasping what must be done in a burst of understanding. The elements of an existing situation suddenly seem to rearrange themselves, and learning occurs in a rush. This experience, called *insight*, involves the kind of cognitive learning that helps humans and even some animals to solve problems. Chimpanzees, for example, seem to learn by insight when they use available objects such as boxes or poles to obtain food that is beyond easy reach. Instead of learning by trial and error, they seem to ponder the situation and then spring into action when the solution comes to them.

Cognitive scientists apply this principle to the idea of "learning to learn." Once someone grasps the principle that underlies a problem, solving other problems that involve the same principle will be easier. For instance, many board games are similar, and when a child masters one game, then learning a second, and a third becomes progressively easier.

Insight enables a person to draw upon past experiences to solve new problems. Cognitive learning, of which insight is one variety, puts past experience to work in helping to solve new problems.

Concept Learning

Concept learning is another area of interest to researchers. Concepts involve the classification of things according to their shared features. As children grow, they learn thousands of concepts. The concept of "fruit," for example, includes oranges, apples, and grapes, while the concept of "color" includes green, red, and blue. Concepts greatly streamline the thought process.

Concept learning applies to humans more than other animals, since verbal ability governs much conceptual thinking. Nevertheless, a recent experiment proved that even pigeons have a limited ability to grasp concepts: the birds were shown pictures of cats, cars, chairs, humans, or flowers. They were taught to peck a corresponding button for each picture. When a new set of pictures was shown to them, the pigeons pecked the right button in each category 70% of the time. By learning what characteristics each of these categories had in common, they had learned to recognize the differences among cats, cars, chairs, humans, and flowers.

Learned Helplessness

Work in the laboratory has taught scientists a lot about principles of learning. In order to be useful, however, the knowledge they have gained must be applicable to real-life situations. In recent years, learning research has come to improve people's lives in two ways.

Psychologist Martin Seligman of the University of Pennsylvania has done extensive research showing that depressed feelings can be based on experience. *Learned helplessness* is his term for the condition wherein animals or humans simply stop trying to improve a bad situation and become depressed, believing that nothing they do will change their circumstances. Dogs, rats, fish, and humans have all proved susceptible to learned helplessness when confronted with adverse situations beyond their control.

In one of Seligman's experiments involving learned helplessness, groups of people were given word puzzles to solve. The first group was given unsolvable puzzles, a second group was given easy puzzles, and a third group got no puzzles. Later, all three groups were given a second round of puzzles, all of which were easy. The second and third groups solved these second puzzles, while most of the people in the first group did not even try to solve them; they had learned that all efforts were useless and so gave up, reporting that a feeling of depression accompanied their lack of effort.

Seligman became intrigued by the idea that *depression*, a crushing mental condition that affects millions of Americans, can be learned. Seligman believes that the way in which people talk to themselves throughout their daily mental dialogue determines whether they will triumph over or give in to depression. If this pattern of internal dialogue can be learned, it can also be unlearned. Seligman has recently been trying to teach people how to talk themselves through hard times: *learned optimism* is his term for developing a thought system to combat helplessness or despair.

People also learn the perceptions they have of themselves, and in a similar manner, the development of an individual's personality depends in part on his or her experiences. As one Chinese proverb states: "To understand a person, you must know their memories." The next chapter will explore the types of memory common to all people.

CHAPTER 3

PROCESSES OF MEMORY

In order to remember, every person must go through the three stages of learning, storing, and retrieving information. These mental processes operate most conspicuously in the classroom, where students must listen, study, and take tests, but are also at work in driving an automobile, painting a picture, or preparing a meal.

The word *memory* describes many different processes. Specific processes, acting in combination with one another, govern the memory of an odor or a face, of how to sing or tie a shoe. Memory also varies in other ways. Consider, for example, a multiple-choice versus a fill-in-the-blank test. The former requires only that the correct information be recognized; the latter calls for memory to supply information.

People have different memory capacities. One person may have a good memory for facts and figures but little memory of his or her childhood years; another may have good visual memory but no recall for music. Some people process incoming impressions rapidly; others need a lot of time to do so. Some people can recall vast amounts of information in detail without effort; others struggle hard to retain new information. In general, women seem to have a better memory for odors than do men. The list of variations in the formation of memory is endless.

Despite these differences in the ability to process and recall information, each person's brain employs the same mechanism in accomplishing the task of remembering. Anything remembered has gone through three distinct phases: a learning stage, in which information is perceived by the brain; a storage stage, in which information is filed; and a retrieval stage, in which information that has been filed is recovered for use.

SENSORY MEMORY

The 18th-century British writer Samuel Johnson once said that "The true art of memory is the art of attention." Indeed, the attention given to objects, events, and other information largely determines what is and is not remembered. Consciously or not, we notice what is important or striking to us and filter out the rest. (Which is why advertisers try to make their appeals as catchy as possible!)

All human impressions of the outside world enter the mind through the five senses of hearing, sight, touch, taste, and smell. When someone perceives a sight or sound, it lingers in the mind in its original form for only a second or less. The impression that it makes during this time is referred to as *sensory memory*. It is this type of memory that holds the image of the flame momentarily in mind after a match struck in the dark is extinguished.

SHORT-TERM MEMORY (STM)

Some of the impressions made in sensory memory are strong enough to pass into *short-term memory* (STM). STM retains current thoughts—but only for about 20 seconds. It holds new, incoming data as well as thoughts of past experiences, such as recollections of last year's vacation or the batting averages of major-league baseball players. During the moment that they are in conscious thought, these data are considered part of STM.

On the average, STM can hold only about seven items at a time. It is fairly easy to write down five numbers and remember them after a brief look. But recalling ten numbers at once usually proves too much for STM. However, a technique called *chunking* can stretch this limit. Thus, for remembering 12 numbers in a row, such as 149217761812, a person may try separating them into three distinct chunks: 1492, 1776, and 1812. This makes them much easier to recall. The same principle applies to letters. Grouping informationrin this way enables STM to hold more facts at once. However, as the size of each chunk grows, STM holds fewer chunks.

More effort is needed to make new information last longer than 20 seconds. To keep new information in STM for longer than this, an individual must repeat it often. This sort of effort involves *elaborative rehearsal*, purposely thinking about information and associating it with established facts. Thus, when a pencil and paper are not at hand, an individual may voice a telephone number several times after seeing or

When a pencil and paper are not handy, many people repeat a telephone number aloud to themselves in order to remember it. Such repetition keeps the newly acquired information within the realm of short-term memory for a sufficient time to permit using it to dial the telephone number.

hearing it. The term *rote rehearsal* refers to such continued repetition of a fact in order to hold it in STM for a longer period.

LONG-TERM MEMORY (LTM)

Although the holding capacity of STM is limited, the storehouse of *long-term memory* (LTM) is astonishingly vast. An amazing variety of items—both influential and insignificant—are stored in LTM, including facts, ideas, and language, with the latter covering rules of grammar as well as individual words. LTM stores directions and routes, personal history, faces, and the taste of apples.

Transfer to LTM Storage

Like a card catalog in a library, LTM cross-references its vast holdings of facts, faces, and impressions in a great variety of ways. The more often an item of information is cross-referenced, the more likely it is to be retrieved when needed. A basic premise in the study of memory is that the more often an item of information appears or is associated with other items, the easier it is to recall.

The greater the number of associations a person can make between a new item of information and data already in LTM, the more likely that item will be to enter LTM. A student who speaks only English and tries to memorize a poem in Spanish will find that the words seem like gibberish and are hard to recall. But a Spanish-speaking student who tries to memorize the same poem will have greater success. He or she can associate the meaning of the words with specific images, making the task much easier. Items that make no sense to the mind are harder for it to store.

The meaning of a word or other item provides several ways to build cross references for it. For example, an English-speaking student who is studying Spanish and must memorize the word *dia* might try associating it with the word *day*, its English counterpart. To strengthen this association, the student might note that both words start with the letter *D*. Additionally, the student could visualize a bright, sunny day while thinking or saying aloud the word *dia*. These are various ways of rehearsing information.

Because facts can usually be more easily cross-referenced than can experiences, factual memory seems stronger than personal memory. New facts are likely to be related to, and thus supported by, numerous other facts, often of various types, that have already been stored. In contrast, memories of specific moments may be more easily forgotten because they involve only a single point in time. They are associated with the moments that occur before and after them but are rarely connected to other, more distant memories.

Data that have emotional significance are also likely to be processed into LTM. A shocking experience is usually remembered along with the details surrounding it. At such moments, the brain seems to

A photograph of the space shuttle Challenger *just seconds after it exploded on January 28, 1986. The incident was so shocking that many people can still recall what they were doing and where they were when they heard of the disaster. Such vivid recollections are called flashbulb memories.*

take a mental "photograph" of its surroundings. Such vivid, complete recollections are called *flashbulb memories*. For example, many people remember exactly where they were and what they were doing on January 28, 1986, when they first heard that the space shuttle *Challenger* had exploded with seven persons aboard.

Coding for Transfer

Before information can be stored in LTM it must remain in STM long enough to be coded for transfer. Much of the information stored in LTM is based on an underlying pattern of significance. Thus, the words "I grew these tomatoes myself" obviously do not mean that tomatoes sprout from human beings. The statement itself is referred to as the *surface structure* of the idea that the speaker is a successful gardener. A listener would understand this and would store this information without recalling the words themselves. This sort of memory is based on the words' actual meaning, referred to as the *deep structure*.

The coding process also occurs in other ways. Lists of numbers, letters, or both are often stored *phonologically*, according to how they sound when spoken rather than how they look when written. One experiment showed that people who were given a short time to read words but no chance to vocalize them had difficulty remembering them. *Vocalization* and *subvocalization* (saying something silently in one's head) seem to be important keys to the coding of memories. There may be much truth to "Say a word three times and its yours."

Other types of information are not stored phonologically. Maps, graphs, and pictures are more efficiently perceived and stored visually, without verbalization. Likewise, deaf persons rely more heavily on vision to store information.

RETRIEVAL

The social studies teacher calls on Wayne in class and asks him, "What is the capital of Vermont?" Wayne searches his mind. Montgomery? Montreal? It is on the tip of his tongue, but he cannot quite remember

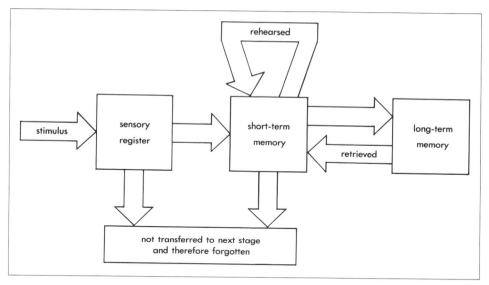

Although information may be registered in short-term memory and properly encoded and transferred to long-term memory, the mind must be able to retrieve it from long-term memory in order for it to be of use.

the city's name. He is searching for *Montpelier*. Such tip-of-the-tongue experiences happen all the time as the mind searches its long-term memory for data it knows it has stored but cannot find. Retrieval is the third, crucial stage of the memory process: data that cannot be retrieved when needed is not very useful.

To get through a typical day, human beings rely on their ability to find thousands of facts at a moment's notice. If incoming information were tossed helter-skelter into a giant mental heap, remembering would be an endless task. It would force the mind to hunt through its 280 quintillion pieces of data whenever it searched its long-term memory, making a simple decision an impossibility. To have a reliable and efficient memory, details must be organized in a way that makes them easy to retrieve. Fortunately, as information enters LTM, the mind classifies and organizes it according to specific principles that make it easier to find later on.

Organization for Retrieval

Scientists have noted several mental processes involved in submitting facts to memory. In 1932, British psychologist Frederick Bartlett observed a phenomenon he called *reconstructive memory*. Bartlett found that most people do not remember accurately the way in which a story was told or an event occurred. When he himself told a story to different students at Cambridge University and asked them to recall the story as they remembered it, he found that they often changed parts of the story or distinctive words or concepts that had been used throughout the story to match their own perceptions. A story about Indians in canoes, for example, was often retold with the words "natives in boats." Bartlett proposed that people's reconstructive memory is formed in such a way that it complies with previous personal experiences. This compliance in reconstructive memory is often used to explain the fact that many people recount personal experiences in such a way as to make themselves look good. They are not lying, but simply remembering incorrectly—and optimistically.

Schemas

Bartlett used his knowledge of reconstructive memory to formulate his *schema theory*: early experiences in life teach the individual to expect that events and actions will continue to occur in the same way. For example, children who have not yet attended school usually feel fearful when they begin to attend. By the end of their first year, however, they know what to expect and how to behave and are much less fearful. They have learned how to follow a daily structure, or scheme, of events.

Schemas work in several ways to help memory. One of these is by directing one's attention. For instance, students in a classroom rapidly learn to listen to the teacher and tune out the playground sounds coming through the window. Schemas also form a basis for storing information. When a person establishes a framework for storing familiar information, he or she is better able to recognize new data and locate it in this framework in relation to similar material already stored there. This process helps to streamline the retrieval process.

Conceptual Hierarchy

In addition to schemas there is a similar type of organization within LTM, called a *conceptual hierarchy*. This helps a person to memorize information by putting it into larger categories or sets. For example, if a student were told to memorize 20 Latin names of plants and animals for a biology test, he or she might first divide the list into animals and plants, then further separate the animals into vertebrates and invertebrates, and so forth, before trying to recall the names of the animals and plants. This system of organizing items into general categories, and then further subdividing them, is an efficient memory device that the human mind uses constantly without realizing it.

Contextual Cues

A recent theory suggests that the memory of an event or piece of information is improved when the individual is surrounded by the same environmental cues that existed when it was learned. Experiments used to test this theory have largely involved studying and test-taking techniques.

In 1986, psychologist Steven Smith, now at Texas A & M University, performed an experiment with undergraduate volunteers at the University of Oklahoma. He taught students a list of 40 words and two days later asked them to recall the words. A group of students for whom Smith had played music by Mozart while teaching them the words were better able to recall the words when the Mozart music was played again.

Students who learned the words to the tune of the Mozart music and were then asked to recall them while listening to soft jazz did not score as high, nor did those students who learned with music but were tested in silence. It appears that environmental cues that exist during a learning experience may activate the memory for the learned information and aid in its recall.

FORGETTING

Several theories attempt to explain why people forget. The *decay theory*, which suggests that the passage of time causes memories to weaken, was tested by asking subjects to remember three specific letters, such as *G, N,* and *X*. The subjects were then asked to count backward, a task that would take time without influencing the ability to remember letters. When more than 20 seconds were allowed to lapse, the subjects were unable to recall the letters. This showed that the passage of time causes memory to weaken, a form of forgetting.

Because STM can hold only a limited amount of information, it can run more efficiently than LTM. Once information leaves STM it is probably lost forever unless an attempt has been made to submit it to LTM first. This, however, can have its beneficial side, since much of the information encountered in life is unnecessary and probably unwanted as far as LTM is concerned.

Once information has entered LTM, it is unlikely to be forgotten as a result of decay; the loss of memory from LTM is caused by another kind of forgetting process, referred to as interference.

Interference Theory

The *interference theory* proposes that interruption of the thought process, rather than decay with the passage of time, causes forgetting. Interference might occur in one of two ways. When new material

Proactive interference can create difficulty when one is learning new information. An example of this occurs with a computer program that is so familiar to an individual that it interferes with the learning of a new program.

interferes with the retrieval of previously stored information, *retroactive interference* is said to take place. Thus, a person who is learning a new computer program may become unable to recall an older program that he or she has used for years. The opposite phenomenon, known as *proactive interference*, occurs when old information is so ingrained in memory that replacing it with new information becomes difficult.

Interference occurs most often when new and old information are similar. Retroactive interference seems to be caused by a shortage of storage space: new information pushes out the old and fills its place. Proactive interference involves retrieval problems: perhaps the old and new information are so similar that they are called up by the same retrieval cue, but the old information comes to mind automatically because it was learned first and remembered longer.

Repression

Another theory of forgetting springs from Freud's theory of *repression*. Freud suggested that people repress unwanted or frightening memories. A child who has witnessed a terrible accident, for example, may completely block out any conscious memory of it. Although the experience remains in the child's mind, it cannot be recalled because it is

The Austrian physician Sigmund Freud, renowned as the founder of psychoanalysis, suggested that people repress, or bury, unwanted and fearful memories.

buried deep in the *subconscious*. In extreme cases, the child may forget other events from the same period as the frightening event, such as information learned in school on the day of the accident.

False Memories

In addition to being lost or buried, memories may also be simply incorrect. In the early 1980s, psychologist Elizabeth Loftus of the University of Washington performed a series of experiments to test the accuracy of memory. She found that the power of suggestion can lead people to remember incorrectly, thereby casting doubt on the reliability of eyewitness testimony given in court.

One of Loftus's experiments, conducted in a bus station, involved a woman who was instructed to leave her bags alone for a few minutes. Upon returning, she was to act as if a tape recorder had been stolen from her luggage. Although no tape recorder had actually existed, several eyewitnesses described the recorder in great detail. The witnesses had come to believe that they really had seen a tape recorder. This and other research has now led trial judges to remind juries that eyewitnesses can make mistakes.

Despite its many quirks and mysteries, the human mind manages to run smoothly with an amazing degree of speed, accuracy, and flexibility. The next chapter will examine the mechanisms that enable the brain to continually maintain this high level of performance in both memory and learning.

CHAPTER 4

MECHANISMS OF MEMORY

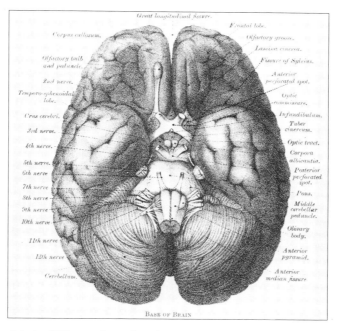

A late-19th-century drawing of the brain viewed from its base, taken from J. Ryland Whitaker's book Anatomy of the Brain and Spinal Cord.

An idea, a nightmare, or an emotion cannot be touched, tasted, or heard, yet all of them result from specific physical processes. All mental activity has a physical basis, with electrical and chemical reactions occurring constantly in the billions of nerve cells of the brain.

Neuroscientists, specialists who study the brain and nervous system, have many questions: where does the adult brain—a blob of Jell-O-like matter that weighs about three pounds—keep the trillions of memories it is capable of holding? Which brain regions govern memory and learning processes? Questions outnumber answers, but scientists are beginning to understand what happens in the brain when a memory forms.

PENFIELD'S PERMANENT MEMORY

Many early ideas about specific brain functions came in the 1940s and 1950s from Wilder Penfield, a Montreal neurosurgeon who worked with epileptic patients. Penfield hoped that he could cure his patients' epilepsy by finding and removing the disturbed part of the brain that caused the condition.

Before performing surgery on an epileptic patient, Penfield anesthetized only the part of the patient's head on which the surgery was to be done, so that the patient could remain conscious without feeling pain. Because brain tissue itself does not experience pain, Penfield was able to use a weakly charged electrode to stimulate various parts of the

In the mid-20th century, neurosurgeon Wilder Penfield discovered that stimulating certain areas of the brain with electrodes enabled patients to recall long-forgotten memories in vivid detail.

brain while his patients were awake. In this way, he discovered that certain areas of the brain activate corresponding parts of the body.

Penfield also discovered that stimulating certain brain areas enabled patients to recall, in extremely vivid detail, long-forgotten memories. One young woman described hearing the voice of a woman who had once lived in her neighborhood. When the electrode was placed at another point, she reported memories of a traveling circus with wagons hauling large animals. These results suggest that even very early experiences, no matter how insignificant, remain in the brain.

Today, the theory that everything ever encountered is stored somewhere in the brain is less popular than it used to be. For one thing, some of the memories reported by Penfield's patients were later revealed to be inaccurate. Also, researchers have more recently found that the brain's structures cannot always be assigned simple, individual functions. Nevertheless, specific brain areas have proved to play a major role in certain aspects of memory and learning.

BRAIN AREAS AND FUNCTIONS

The area that most people picture when they hear the word *brain* is the *cerebral cortex*, the center of human learning, thinking, talking, and remembering. Often simply called the cortex, it is the most recently evolved part of the brain and more highly developed in humans than in other animals. It is the part of the brain responsible for storing long-term memory.

The cortex contains about 80% of the brain's weight. It appears to take up very little space, but its many folds of tissue would take up 400 square inches of a tabletop if stretched out. These folds allow the cortex to have such a large surface area, and therefore large numbers of nerve cells, in the small space of the skull.

The cortex includes the *forebrain*, the part of the brain positioned behind the forehead. The forebrain is divided into two halves, called *cerebral hemispheres*, each of which is responsible for certain functions. Each hemisphere contains four paired lobes, each of them paired with the corresponding lobe in the other hemisphere. Each pair of lobes

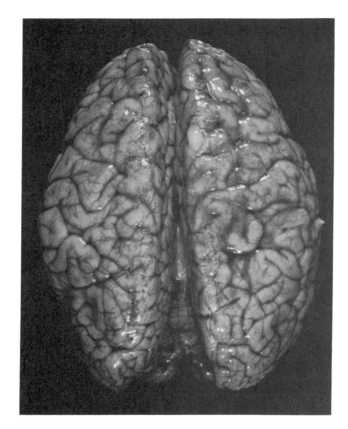

A view of the brain from above, showing the many folds of the cerebral cortex and its division into two hemispheres.

controls specific activities. The *frontal lobes* are responsible for such uniquely human traits as self-awareness, planning, and initiative, although other parts of the brain are important in putting these abilities to use.

The Thalamus

In 1960, the thin blade of a fencing sword pierced through a young man's nose and into his brain. Now known in scientific circles as N.A., this young man became the subject of much interest to Larry Squire at the University of California Medical School in San Diego. His brain injury enabled scientists to identify brain structures that govern memory and learning.

N.A.'s injury affected a part of the forebrain called the *thalamus* (meaning "couch" in Greek and so named because the cerebral hemispheres rest upon it). The thalamus is an important brain structure because it receives all incoming sensory information (except that of smell) and encodes it before sending it on to the cortex for further processing or storage in the form of long-term memory. When the thalamus is damaged, new data can no longer pass into LTM in the cortex.

Because of this, N.A. lives in an eternal, disconnected present. He can meet someone in the morning and have no memory of that person in the afternoon. He cannot understand television shows, because during each commercial he forgets the plot. Yet he does remember his past before the accident and can still use his short-term memory. Thus the thalamus seems to be involved in encoding information in short-term memory before transferring and filing long-term memories for storage in the cortex.

The Limbic System

The thalamus also connects the cortex to another important brain center, the *limbic system*. This area, located in the center of the brain, transfers information to long-term memory and balances raw sensations with rational thought.

Two parts of the limbic system are important in transferring data from STM to LTM: the *hippocampus* (Greek for "seahorse" and so named because it is roughly shaped like one) and the *amygdala* (Greek for "almond," also named for its shape). Once the data is stored, however, the hippocampus and amygdala are no longer needed.

Although the hippocampus and amygdala perform similar tasks that involve associative memory skills, they operate by distinct mechanisms. The hippocampus is considered responsible for recalling associations in spatial relations. Thus, for example, it allows someone who has left their car keys at home to envision the exact spot where they probably still are. In fact, the hippocampus is involved in many important brain functions, including emotion and motivation, as well as memory and learning.

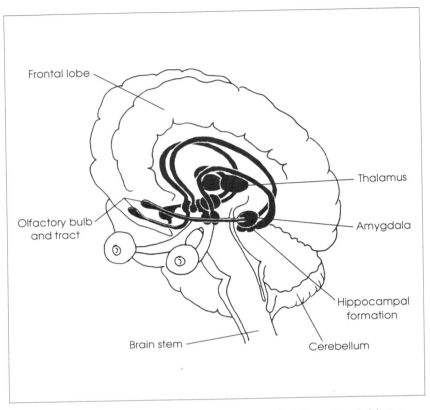

Frontal lobe

Thalamus

Olfactory bulb
and tract

Amygdala

Hippocampal
formation

Brain stem

Cerebellum

Located deep in the center of the brain, the limbic system's hippocampus and amygdala, like the thalamus, transfer information to be stored in long-term memory.

The amygdala is responsible for associating memories formed in the different senses. It also links memories with emotions. As an example of this, it permits us to visually recall the round shape and bright color of an orange from the mere odor of an orange. It also permits the odor of the orange to recall a pleasant trip to an orange grove.

As with the thalamus, removal of the hippocampus and amygdala prevents the recall of new information by preventing the transfer of new information into LTM. However, removal of these structures does not interfere in the recall of events that occurred before their removal.

The Olfactory Nerve

The most intense associative sense seems to be that of smell. A simple odor has the ability to recall memories instantly and in great detail. For example, the odor of cinnamon rolls may suddenly summon childhood memories of a visit to a grandmother's house, bringing back specific experiences as well as a general mood. An odor can also bring back the appearance, sound, feel, and taste of an object—all in equally vivid detail.

Unlike other senses, smell is not transferred through the thalamus before it reaches the cortex. Instead, the *olfactory nerve*, the structure inside the nose that detects and carries odors, is linked directly to the brain's limbic system. It can thus signal the cortex in less than a second.

THE CEREBELLUM AND PROCEDURAL MEMORY

Most people view memory as the recall of facts and events, an ability often referred to as *declarative memory*. However, recent studies have identified another essential type of memory, which involves a different area of the brain.

Procedural memory is used to learn skills and actions that can be repeated automatically without conscious thought. These skills often involve physical activities, such as riding a bicycle or throwing a ball. Learning through this type of memory requires repetitive practice.

The *cerebellum* is the area of the brain responsible for learning repetitive actions and holding them in procedural memory in both humans and animals. Located at the rear and near the base of the brain, the cerebellum is a cauliflower-shaped structure that controls movement. It maintains balance, controls muscle tone, and coordinates the direction, force, and rate of movement. It is constantly active, ensuring that the body is running smoothly. Conscious, or voluntary, motor activity begins in the cortex, which sends instructions for a particular activity to the cerebellum. The cerebellum then translates these instructions into specific signals that it sends to the muscles needed for performing the activity.

Memory has always intrigued humankind, and neuroscientists have made great strides in understanding it. Although scientists now know more than ever before about the brain's mechanisms, many questions remain to be answered. The next chapter will explore recent advances in the study of memory.

CHAPTER 5

THE SEARCH FOR THE MEMORY TRACE

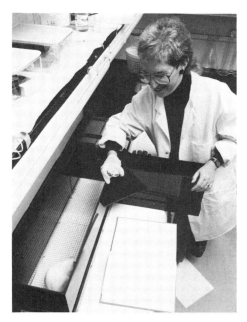

Studying an experimental drug that enhances memory by acting directly on the neurotransmitter acetylcholine, psychologist Jacqueline Crawley times a rat's progress through a T-maze.

One of the most intense quests in science today is the search for the *memory trace*, the physical explanation for memory and learning. Many questions focus on the true nature of memory: is it fleeting or permanent? When the brain gains a piece of knowledge, what occurs in its cells? Does a memory create a lasting impression that changes the brain's structure, or does it dissolve forever, never to be known again?

THE ENGRAM

Toward the end of his life American psychologist Karl Lashley wrote, "I sometimes feel, in reviewing the evidence . . . that learning just is not possible." From 1920 through the 1950s, Lashley devoted himself to hunting for the memory trace in the nervous system. He used the word engram to refer to this neuronal basis for memory and learning. But decades of research left him frustrated, with little understanding of how learned knowledge is stored.

Lashley first believed that a given memory is stored in a very specific area of the brain, perhaps in a small group of cells. His plan to find this area was simple: he would train rats to run a maze, surgically remove some small part of their brain while carefully documenting which section he removed, then return them to the maze. Lashley eventually expected to find rats that had lost their recall of how to run the maze. In knowing which part of the brain was missing, he would know where the maze-running memory had been stored.

But the rats never seemed to forget. No matter what part or how much of their brain was missing, their maze-running memories survived. Baffled at first by the meaning of this, Lashley finally decided that memories are not stored in specific brain cells. Instead, he suggested, a single memory is stored throughout the brain.

These views prevailed throughout the scientific community for years, but recent research has thrown his conclusions into doubt. Many scientists now argue that rats who learn to run a maze probably make simultaneous use of various sense cues—such as sight, smell, and spatial layout—to guide them. Destroying the brain's memory for visual cues may still leave the rat with smell cues to help it navigate.

CELL ASSEMBLIES

In 1949, Donald Hebb, a founder of physiological psychology, originated a theory about the brain and learning that is still current. Hebb theorized that *cell assemblies*, groups of nerve cells that associate with and affect each other, are the basis of memory storage in the brain. Each sort of experience is stored in a certain type of cell assembly, and as a person has new experiences, the cell assemblies begin to make interconnected associations.

These associations occur through *circuits*, the familiar pathways formed between groups of nerve cells in the brain. Circuits are formed when nerve cells and the minuscule gaps, known as *synapses*, that separate these cells become active. This excitability is short-lived in STM, where these changes occur only briefly. Yet in LTM, the activity between cells and synapses lasts long enough to permanently change the structure of the cells themselves. One theory of how the brain's memory capacity develops suggests that as circuits spread out to make new associations, they lead to the creation of new cell assemblies in previously underutilized sections of the cortex.

One example of how circuits may lead to the creation of new cell assemblies can be found in the way a child learns. A youngster's first encounter with a puppy may leave only a visual impression of a large

A child's overall perception of a dog may develop from a number of encounters, each causing impressions to be stored in separate cell assemblies that become connected in a circuit. In this way, new experiences become linked, in memory, to those of the past.

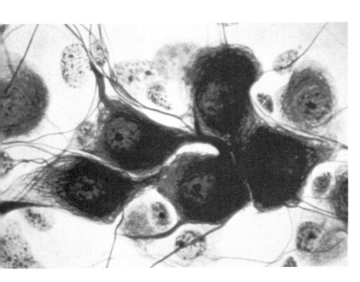

This photomicrograph of neurons taken from an 11-day-old mouse brain and magnified 200 times shows the complex network formed by the cells' thick dendrites and long axons.

creature with big ears. This impression would be stored in a certain cell assembly for sight. The next encounter may add the sound of barking to the former picture of the dog, and this image would be stored in a cell assembly for sound. A circuit would then form to connect the two impressions—visual and auditory—of the dog. Eventually, the child forms a composite picture of all the images pertaining to dogs, and new experiences become interlinked, via circuits, to previous ones.

NEURONS

Although Hebb devised these theories in the 1940s, it was not until fairly recently, after scientists gained more understanding of the brain's cells, that Hebb's picture came to be seen as accurate. While the body is composed entirely of cells, only certain types of cells are responsible for transmitting information throughout the nervous system. These nerve cells are known as *neurons*. They enable the body to relay information to the brain and vice versa.

Of the human body's billions of nerve cells, approximately 70% (about 100 billion) are located in the brain. Although neurons are very small, scientists have found a valuable way to study them. Neurons operate on electrical impulses that can be measured and traced.

The Neuron's Path

Neurons basically remain at rest until a stimulus occurs, and then they become extremely active. In order to test neurons, researchers have created an *electrode*, a minuscule tube that delicately enters a neuron's *membrane*, or outer wall. Electrodes are designed to serve two functions at once: they send an electrical stimulus into the cell and then send the neuron's signals back to a machine to record them.

This task sounds simpler than it actually is. Placing an electrode in a neuron requires painstaking patience, but one electrode is not enough. Each neuron is only a single link in the long pathway of neurons transmitting a message. To map the cells' interactions, scientists must study several at one time, placing electrodes into a series of neurons.

Gaps in the Path

The pathway created by a series of neurons does not take the form of a long, continuous road. A neuronal path could be compared to a trail of stepping-stones with space between each rock. These gaps between neurons are the synapses described earlier. They play an essential role in relaying messages about memories and current sensations.

Synapses are important because they create barriers of space that help neurons avoid sending messages where they are not intended to go. If the cells in the brain touched each other directly, every piece of information would spread to every other part of the brain and body. The different parts of the brain would no longer perform the separate functions that control and direct thoughts and actions. Fortunately, the synaptic gaps separate cells, limiting the number of pathways a certain type of message can follow.

Messengers

How does each neuron send information across the synapse to the next neuron? To understand this process, one must realize that, despite its minuscule size, each neuron contains a world of its own. Inside each neuron are many types of *molecules*, the building blocks of matter.

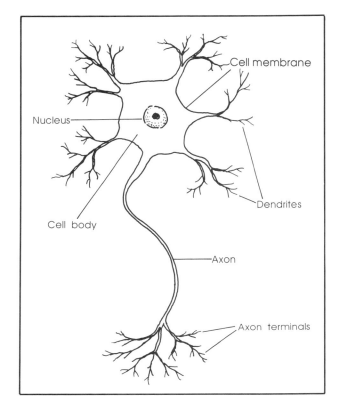

Neurons are like other kinds of cells in that they have a cell membrane, a nucleus, and cytoplasm. However, they are distinguished by the long process known as an axon extending from their cell body, by the branchlike extensions known as dendrites, and by their secretion of chemical components called neurotransmitters. All of these properties enable the neuron to communicate with other neurons.

When a neuron receives a signal, its molecules begin to react. They set off a series of electrical actions that push more molecules toward the neuron's *axon*, the part of the cell that sends outgoing messages to other cells. When enough molecules accumulate at the tip of the axon, they push open a small gate that allows special molecules to escape.

These special molecules, called *neurotransmitters*, form a chemical substance that flows across the synapse toward another neuron along the pathway. This new neuron has a group of armlike extensions, called *dendrites*, that reach out to receive the neurotransmitter messages. Once the new neuron receives the chemical signal, it converts the signal back into electrical impulses that create a molecular reaction in the new cell. In the same way that the previous neuron passed the message through its cell, the new neuron also passes the message in electrical form down to its own axon. Thus the message travels along the pathway from one neuron to the next in a chain reaction.

The Importance of Neurotransmitters

But how do neurons know which pathway to follow and which axons and dendrites to use to relay information to the right place? Scientists are still exploring this question, but currently they believe that the neurotransmitters play a crucial part in this process.

There are many types of neurotransmitters, each composed of molecules with a different chemical basis. Each neurotransmitter helps relay a message that can be received only by certain neurons that can read the chemical language specific to that neurotransmitter. A stimulus that a person encounters frequently makes a stronger, longer-lasting impression because the neural pathways are well established. A stimulus that a person rarely encounters may have no lasting effect because it fails to establish a neural pathway.

These pathways are important for both learning and memory. Experiences that are repeated are more likely to become permanently stored and are more easily retrieved. For example, even after

To investigate the permanent physical changes in neural structures during learning, Eric Kandel of Columbia University chose to experiment with Aplysia. These sea slugs have larger and fewer neurons than humans, yet are able to learn and remember, making them ideal organisms for the study of these two functions.

people graduate from school, they usually continue to use skills such as addition and subtraction, strengthening those neural pathways through the brain. Conversely, most people barely remember algebra and geometry because those subjects are seldom reviewed when school is over.

Recent research has pinpointed *acetylcholine* and *glutamate* as significant neurotransmitters for memory and learning. Acetylcholine appears to communicate to the neurons about the arrival of a stimulus. As it carries this message along the neural pathway, it stimulates the neurons, enabling learning to occur.

Glutamate activates a similar type of communication between neurons in the hippocampus. These messages often produce long-term neuronal changes that may be the cause of memory. Despite inroads made in understanding the function of these neurotransmitters, so many chemicals are involved in memory and learning that scientists have not yet documented all of them.

The study of the neurophysiology involved in memory and learning has far to go, yet these findings strengthen the theory that behavior is caused by a combination of physical and environmental factors. The brain constantly adapts, incorporating physical changes in response to the learning that accompanies everyday experience. The next chapter will look at how memory and learning develop throughout each person's lifetime.

CHAPTER 6

ACROSS
A LIFETIME

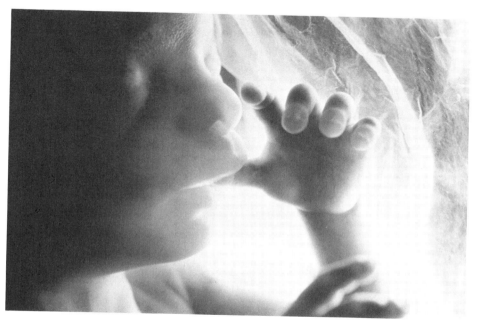

A photograph of a fetus in its third trimester of development, taken in the womb. Although most people recall very little of their years before the age of three or four, recent theories propose that learning actually begins in the womb.

Most people cannot recall much about their childhood, especially the years before they were three or four. In fact, many people are not certain whether their earliest memories are their own or simply stories they have heard from older family members.

Yet this lack of memory does not mean that youngsters do not learn or remember what they learn. It is a fact that newborns know much less than a one-year-old does. And within five years, most

Claiming that her unborn infant responds to sound, the woman in this photograph pipes music to the baby via headphones. Some mothers read to their unborn children, hoping that it will help them learn to read with greater ease.

children accumulate enough knowledge to start school without much difficulty. Certainly, a great deal of learning takes place long before a child enters school.

EARLY LEARNING

Babies begin learning as early as their first day in the world, and recent theories propose that they may even be learning before this. Some enthusiastic parents read to their infant while it is still in the womb, with the hope that it will one day have an easier time learning to read. In a 1986 study by Dr. Anthony J. DeCasper, a psychologist at the University of North Carolina, expectant mothers repeatedly read a particular passage aloud during their last six weeks of pregnancy. After the babies were born, they showed a preference for this same passage.

As infants grow physically and in their degree of coordination, their central nervous system also develops. The brain grows rapidly, reaching three-quarters of its adult size before a child is two years old. The brain also develops complex connections between nerve cells and in its various regions.

Unlike the young of other animals, such as kittens and puppies, human infants are born with the ability to see and hear, although these senses are not yet well formed. Many scientists believe that in order for these senses to develop to their full potential, sense perceptions must be established within a certain period of time and before a certain age. The age varies, depending on which of the senses is being considered. Cases of persons who are born blind and later develop vision tend to confirm this view; such persons never seem to acquire certain visual skills that are usually developed early in life.

To have full perceptual skills, youngsters must learn pattern perception, distance and depth perception, and object perception. They must also acquire skills in hearing, touch, taste, and smell. With these abilities, a child can distinguish components of the world around him or her.

MEMORY AS A LEARNED PROCESS

Why do adults remember so little of their early childhood? For many years the leading theory on this subject was Freud's theory of *infantile amnesia*. Freud believed that early memories were so charged with primitive sexual feelings that people blocked them out of their conscious minds. More recently, psychologists have come to believe that remembering is a learned process.

Because very young infants perceive every event as new and equally important, nothing is routine to them. As they gain experience, however, they become sufficiently familiar with events and situations that they can begin to put them into recognizable and definable categories.

Family routines are the most frequently and clearly remembered impressions from early childhood. These repeated patterns allow not only categorization but also an opportunity for internal replay to strengthen memory. A child's ability to recognize a routine generally does not appear until age three—the earliest age to which adults can look back for memories.

Before children reach age five, most of their memory skills work toward assimilating new information. A child concentrates on learning how something is done rather than where or when it was learned. This type of focus decreases the number of distinct events that a child will recall. Additionally, external sensory cues are perhaps the only devices that trigger memory in youngsters.

Around the age of five, children first begin to develop an awareness of the past and a time line on which to locate memories of events. Learning language also greatly aids memory. It gives children a way to associate similar objects and experiences and a way to store this knowledge according to schemas. As their memories become based on chronological, internal schemes of memory, children lose the earlier type of memory based on sense-oriented reference points.

By the age of seven, children use language to string events together like a story, with a beginning, middle, and end. When they enter school, they begin to acquire more devices to help them remember, such as rhyming rules that teach the laws of grammar. As children grow even older, they begin to understand the value of memory and consciously try to submit information to it.

ADULT LEARNING AND MEMORY

Although intelligence is thought to begin its decline around the age of 20, because of the loss of brain cells, some studies suggest that humans show no marked changes in their mental capacity until they are at least in their fifties. With continuing research, even these studies are being cast into doubt, and scientists are offering much more optimistic reports about aging and intelligence. Nevertheless, many people continue to fear the loss of memory that accompanies age.

Fewer than 10% of people aged 65 or older ever suffer memory loss as the result of an illness such as *Alzheimer's disease*. Rather, everyone

With aging, all persons experience the type of memory loss known as age-associated memory impairment. But about 10% of people aged 65 or over suffer from other, more debilitating conditions, such as Alzheimer's disease.

experiences a certain amount of forgetting with age, which should be understood as a natural process. Health care workers refer to the natural memory loss associated with aging as *age-associated memory impairment* (AAMI). One study showed that more than 65% of persons over age 75 suffer from some type of memory loss that would be considered normal.

Normal memory loss is not a complete loss of recall, but simply a failure to remember past events and facts related to them. And contrary to popular belief, older people can continue to learn. Often, the only impediment to continued learning by elderly people is their need for extra time to process memories. Thus, when groups of both old and young people were asked to memorize lists of different items in a study done by Drs. Rolf H. Morge and David Hultsch of the Pennsylvania State University, the older subjects did not at first seem to recall the lists as well as did the younger ones. But when given more time to retrieve the newly learned information from memory, the older people greatly improved their performance.

Other studies indicate that humans appear to have at least three types of long-term memory, and that the process of normal aging affects only one of these, known as *episodic memory*. The two remaining types of memory are unaffected. These are *implicit memory*, which refers to the memory of motor skills, and *semantic memory*, which involves the knowledge of vocabulary and facts. Both implicit and semantic memory appear to remain intact among elderly persons.

Episodic memory, the type of memory that is lost among elderly persons, mainly involves the ability to recall past events. Scientists report that the strongest decline in episodic memory occurs at about the age of 70, although it may also appear sooner. Experts often attribute the decline in episodic memory to retirement, when people are no longer required to use this skill as often.

Scientists also wonder why elderly people seem to recall memories of events that happened long ago better than they do more recent personal experiences. David Mitchell, a psychologist at Southern Methodist University, proposes that this is because older memories are mentally repeated so often as a person passes through life that they eventually take the same form as facts and thus enter semantic memory. Each time these facts are recalled, they are further cemented into semantic memory.

AGING AND THE BRAIN

Research shows that today's 65-year-olds are mentally sharper than those of former generations. Perhaps improvements in nutrition and education are responsible for this. Nevertheless, as people age, their brains continue to change physically. Thousands of nerve cells in the adult brain ordinarily disappear every day, and they are not replaced by new cells, as are the cells of most other tissues. Beginning at the age of 20 years, human brains begin to shrink, losing approximately 1 gram

A drawing of a cross-section of a blocked artery that normally carries blood from the heart to the body. In their quest for possible explanations for age-related memory loss, some scientists suggest that as arteries harden with age, some become obstructed, like the one shown here, thus limiting blood flow to the brain. This, in turn, impairs memory and other functions of the brain.

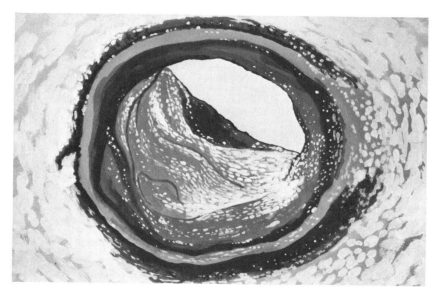

of weight per year. The fissures of the cortex widen and deepen, and the cavities within the brain enlarge.

During the natural process of aging, the frontal lobes, which are responsible for episodic memory, decay more rapidly than other brain areas. Sensory abilities also suffer, which may hinder a person's initial perceptions of a situation or item of information. This decline in perception may limit the information that enters the sensory receptors, hence reducing its chance of entering even STM.

Recent theories have attempted to explain the natural loss of memory that accompanies aging. One theory suggests that *arteries*, the vessels that carry blood from the heart to the body, undergo a process in which their walls become hardened and rigid over the years. This hardening gradually interferes with blood flow to the brain, thus slowing mental activity. In addition, the generally lower level of physical energy of older persons may slow the brain's activity. Newer theories, now being investigated, link memory loss to an age-related depletion of neurotransmitter substances from the brain.

Memory Maintenance

Scientists investigating memory are now offering alternatives to the view that memory loss is an inevitable and natural accompaniment to aging. Believing that older people can improve their memories through practice, some of these scientists are beginning to teach what are called "mental strengthening techniques." One of these techniques, known as *methods of loci*, resembles the memory houses used by the ancient Greeks. It involves using visual skills to aid memory by linking items to be remembered with familiar places. Memorizing a shopping list, for example, might call for picturing one's living room with milk on the bookshelf, bread on the sofa, apples on the end table, and cookies on the chair—an unusual picture that one is likely to recall.

Memory experts have also noticed that excessive concern about memory loss can worsen the problem by causing anxiety, which often interferes with normal memory processes. Too much stress can even make a person unable to think clearly. Experts have recently begun teaching relaxation techniques to help persons who worry about

In the misplaced-objects test, Thomas Crook evaluated the effects
of drugs designed to help older people maintain sharper memories.
Each subject was asked to place two items into each of 12 rooms dis-
played on a computer screen. After a measured time, the subjects
returned to their computer screens and tried to remember where
they had placed each item.

memory loss. Relaxation creates comfort, which reduces stress and makes remembering easier.

In a Stanford University experiment on the effects of relaxation on memory, subjects were helped to relax physically before trying to memorize matching names and faces. These subjects remembered 69% of the information they were given, compared to 44% recalled by those who did not have time to relax beforehand. The impairment of memory by stress has been linked to the body's production of *adrenaline*, a hormone released during stress. High doses of adrenaline have also been found to impair memory in experiments with rats, while low doses seem to help the animals remember.

Modern advances in medical science offer great hope that aging will no longer have to mean severe memory loss. Meanwhile, scientists are still trying to distinguish the learning and memory capabilities that are present at birth from those that are acquired. By understanding these differences, experts hope to learn which aspects of memory can be changed, and perhaps improved upon, and which cannot. The next chapter will examine this question in greater detail.

CHAPTER 7

THE GREAT
DEBATE

The conditions under which a child is raised affect his or her personality and intelligence. But scientists debate among themselves whether environmental factors are more important to a child's development than genetic traits, or vice versa.

A hotly debated question fuels the study of memory and learning: which is more important in shaping people's characters and intelligence—the experiences they have or the genetic qualities they inherit? This question has been termed the nature versus nurture debate, with *nature* referring to genetic factors and *nurture* describing the effect of learning.

Throughout history, occasional reports have surfaced of infants raised either by animals or in complete isolation from other humans.

Scholars and scientists view these cases as rare opportunities to obtain information about human nature in its purest form, uncontaminated by the socializing effect of other people.

In India in 1920, a missionary named Joseph Singh and some native villagers discovered two little girls living in a wolf den in the jungle. The mother wolf was nursing the girls, along with two wolf cubs. The girls and the wolf cubs were cuddled together in a ball, and the girls fought violently when the intruders separated them from their wolf family.

No one knew how the two girls, about three and five years old, came to be in the wolf den. Joseph Singh and his wife ran an orphanage some 50 miles away, where they took the girls. Mrs. Singh cleaned the children up and named them Amala and Kamala. Because for a long time they behaved more like wolves than humans, they were kept in a large cage, separate from other children.

Among other wolflike traits, the two girls were suspicious of people, snarling and baring their teeth if they felt threatened. They walked on all fours and spoke no human language. Raw meat was the only thing they ate, gobbling it like dogs from a bowl on the floor. They seemed to see better by night than by day, and after dark they often paced in their cage, howling loudly.

Amala died within a year after being found, but Kamala lived to be 14 years old. During that time, the Singhs did everything possible to civilize her. After three years she learned to walk upright but remained most comfortable when on all fours. She learned to like vegetables, bread, and sweets, but never as much as raw meat. After five years she spoke 30 words, including "mama," "papa," "I," and "eat." When Kamala died of typhoid fever at the age of 14, she was speaking in short sentences and called Mrs. Singh "Mama." But the pull of her wolfish past remained strong, and those who saw Kamala always found her a disturbing mix of animal and human.

LEARNING TO SPEAK

The nature versus nurture debate often focuses on humankind's unique ability to speak. Scientists and linguists want to understand the mechanism behind a child's ability to speak so quickly. Children begin to make cooing sounds at two months of age, use intonation at four to six months, and by the end of their first year they imitate others' sounds in order to get attention. Children say their first words around their first birthday and six to eight months later begin to produce one-word sentences. Within three years of their birth, most children can speak in full sentences.

Applying his theories on conditioning to children's learning of language, B. F. Skinner proposed that the process is one of trial and error: adults reward children when they make sounds that resemble words.

In their second year, as children begin to distinguish themselves from others, they begin to use possessive words, such as "mine" or "Daddy's." They especially enjoy naming things and begin applying words they already know to objects for which they have not yet learned names. The two- and three-word sentences that children begin to form during their third year usually lack prepositions and articles. These more subtle aspects of speech are inserted to create more complete, complex sentences by the age of three or four. At this age children also learn to use the past tense and begin to ask more questions.

Conditioning

B. F. Skinner, the scientist who developed theories on conditioning, proposed that his ideas also applied to the learning of language. He believed that when infants coo or babble in sounds that resemble words, adults *reinforce*, or reward them. As the child grows older, this reinforcement grows more precise. For example, when a child first says "mama," his mother cuddles him as a reward. Other adults also applaud these efforts. But an older child who says "mama" to an aunt will be ignored rather than rewarded—until the child learns the correct word. Thus, children seem to learn to talk by trial and error.

Studies indicate that a child's social environment is important in its learning of speech. Babies brought up in institutions without supportive adults to reward their efforts babble at the expected age but take longer to talk than children raised by a family. Similarly, deaf children, who babble but cannot hear their own noise or imitate others, need special training to learn the skills of speech.

An Internal Device

Opponents of the idea that language is conditioned argue that reinforcement alone is not enough to teach language with the speed, accuracy, and originality that children show in learning it. They support an alternative theory that holds that children are born with an *internal device* that interprets the adult speech surrounding them. This device enables youngsters to perceive basic grammatical rules, to understand what they hear, and to form sentences. Universal to all humans, the device offers infants a type of map to help them approach the rules of language.

The nature versus nurture debate remains unresolved. Most experts agree that both of these factors are involved in learning language. The human neural structure provides a pathway for learning language, while the environment offers important guidelines for using language to communicate with others.

INTELLIGENCE

The issue of nature versus nurture is particularly important when considering intelligence and personality. How much does environment affect the way in which these traits develop? Scientists have devised several methods for comparing the effects of heredity to those of environment.

Because they cannot take control of human breeding and the early human environment simply for the sake of experimentation, scientists have often instead worked with laboratory animals, especially rats. In doing this, scientists often use *selective breeding*, which enables them to interbreed individual members of an animal species who share a specific trait. It then becomes easier to observe this particular trait in a controlled environment.

Fifty years ago, psychologist Robert C. Tryon at the University of California, Berkeley, began using rats to test the genetics of intelligence. He measured the rats' intelligence according to how accurately and quickly they could learn to run mazes. After separating "maze-bright" and "maze-dull" rats, Tryon then let each of the two kinds breed only with other rats of its group. He found that the maze-dull rats that grew up after a few generations of such breeding made many more mistakes than did maze-bright rats. However, some experts argue that the skills that rats need to run mazes may involve qualities other than intelligence, such as eyesight or reflexes.

Tryon also used experiments with maze-bright rats to test the role of environment. He found that keeping a new generation of young, maze-bright rats in a nonstimulating environment counteracted the effects of selective breeding. When limited to dull surroundings, these rats no longer proved superior to their maze-dull peers who lived in more interesting environments.

In another experiment, Tryon found that when raised together in unstimulating surroundings, both maze-dull and maze-bright rats performed poorly in tests. He also found that maze-dull and maze-bright rats raised together in an especially stimulating environment showed no difference in their ability to conquer mazes. Eventually, Tryon examined the rats' brains and found that those raised in more stimulating environments had heavier brains regardless of their hereditary intelligence.

Humans also become more intelligent when presented with more stimulating surroundings. As early as the 1930s, psychologist H. M. Skeels, while investigating orphanages for the State of Iowa, gave evidence of the importance of environment in children's learning. Skeels observed orphaned children who lived in crowded quarters with few caretakers and little personal attention. Most people assumed that the children had a substandard intelligence. Yet when a few of the girls were removed and taken to adult wards where mature female patients had time to show interest in them, their intelligence quotient (IQ) scores increased remarkably. The IQ of an individual is a numerical value given to his or her intelligence on the basis of a standardized test. A score of 100 represents an average intelligence.

Sociologists cite Skeels's study as evidence that students who come from crowded, lower-income areas and have low grades in school should not automatically be viewed as less intelligent. Rather, their environment does not offer the support and stimulation that children need in order to excel in school and in a career.

A similar idea has been applied to learning in the elderly. Working with rats to explore the effect of environment on learning in the elderly, Marian Cleeves Diamond, a neuroanatomist at the University of California, found that older rats housed in stimulating environments

On the basis of information derived from her studies on learning, Marian Cleeves Diamond proposes that a stimulating environment is important to maintaining the mental power of the elderly.

developed larger brains than did rats kept in isolation with little stimulus. Like Tryon, Diamond found that rats living in enriched environments performed better in mazes than did rats from deprived environments.

On the basis of her findings, Diamond proposes that older people who have stimulating surroundings that evoke their curiosity and challenge their minds are more motivated to develop their mental skills, such as studying and remembering new information. Her research supports the established idea that an active environment is needed to maintain healthy memory skills among elderly persons.

Sex Roles

Much of the nature versus nurture debate has centered on gender. Are the two sexes inherently different, or has each learned only to think differently as a result of its environment? A 1974 study by Eleanor Maccoby at Stanford University and Carol Jacklin at the University of Southern California found no noticeable psychological distinctions between men and women, but did find that their cognitive abilities differed somewhat, with women apparently better at verbal skills and men better at mathematical and visual-spatial abilities.

In contrast, a 1988 study by Alan Feingold at Yale University gave evidence that these mental differences between men and women result from environmental influences. Examining the results of aptitude tests, Feingold noted that the differences between boys' and girls' scores on varied tasks decreased markedly in tests given between 1947 and 1980.

This suggested that with changes in society's expectations of what men and women can do—as has happened in the United States in the period since 1947—differences in the two sexes' cognitive abilities change accordingly. On this basis, it might be said that boys have historically done better at math because of a long-held, stereotyped belief that they are better at this subject, and that the same is true for verbal ability with girls.

Aggression

The word *aggression* refers to behavior that is meant to inflict physical or psychological harm on others. Such behavior is most evident in the violence so often reported in daily newspapers and on television. Some theories support the view that aggression is an inborn behavior, the remnant of a primitive, instinctive reaction to pain and frustration.

During the third game of the National Hockey League's 1990 Stanley Cup championship playoff series, Boston Bruins player Glen Wesley punched the Edmonton Oilers' Craig Simpson. Although Freud suggested that athletic competition could help channel aggression, some studies show that violent sports actually augment destructive behavior in spectators.

Experts agree that frustration and other unpleasant sensations often lead to aggression.

Freud proposed that aggression is an innate response to negative feelings that build up to a climactic point at which they are finally released. He felt that society could help to channel these reactions through various types of competition, such as sports. Some studies suggest that such activities do in fact help to decrease aggressive behavior in persons who might otherwise express an excessive degree of aggression in ways that are socially unacceptable.

Other studies refute Freud's theory that aggression is entirely inborn. These studies suggest that violent activities increase the level of aggression in persons who are normally calm. According to this thesis, contact sports, such as hockey and football, in which forceful physical competition is applauded, may induce both spectators and participants who are not naturally aggressive to become so.

Studies have also indicated that people can be taught to be less aggressive. Thus, when children were divided into two groups, one of which was rewarded for nonaggressive and the other for aggressive behavior, the children who were rewarded for nonaggressive behavior responded more constructively when confronted with a frustrating situation.

Many aspects of thinking and acting can be learned. Yet the extent of such learning is unknown. Scientists and psychologists continue to debate the influences of heredity and environment on intelligence and personality. The next chapter examines how scientists apply new knowledge to fight humanity's oldest foes—illness and aging.

CHAPTER 8

DISORDERS AND DISEASE

Many people enjoy good health and a festive life in their old age.

M any people continue to learn well into their golden years. After retirement, they may involve themselves in community activities and senior citizen groups, travel around the world, start a new business, or settle down to a quiet life of reading and strolling in the park.

Sometimes, however, the later years of life are not golden. In attempting to dress himself in the morning, an elderly man may suddenly be unable to remember whether his socks or his shoes go on his feet first. A wife of 40 years may address her husband with "Hey, Mister!" because she has forgotten his name.

ALZHEIMER'S DISEASE

Severe, permanent memory loss is most often caused by *Alzheimer's disease*. Named for the German doctor who identified it in 1907, Alzheimer's disease is generally signaled by a failure of memory, especially the ability to recall recent events. This is followed by the progressive decay of other mental processes.

The fourth leading cause of death in the United States, Alzheimer's disease usually appears in persons over the age of 65. Because some memory loss is normal with aging, early signs of the disease may go unnoticed. But as it takes hold, its effects are unmistakable.

People with Alzheimer's disease become increasingly disoriented, forgetting how to do simple tasks, such as cooking or dressing. As their

In 1907, German physician Alois Alzheimer diagnosed a disease characterized by severe memory loss. In the United States today, Alzheimer's disease is the fourth leading cause of death.

memory for more recent events fails, they may begin to live in the past. Eventually, even their family and friends become unfamiliar. As the disease continues to affect the brain, its victims lose the ability to walk, talk, and control their bodies.

Although scientists do not yet know the cause of Alzheimer's disease and have no cure for it, they do understand its processes. It acts by attacking the brain's neurons, leaving clumps and tangles of dead or dying neurons scattered through the hippocampus, amygdala, and parts of the cerebral cortex—the areas of the brain that govern memory and learning. A thick, foreign substance grows between the dead and dying cells, and the amount of acetylcholine, one of the neurotransmitters that plays a crucial role in memory and learning, becomes abnormally low.

Recently, researchers have focused their efforts on studying amyloid plaques—areas of diseased tissue in the brain that contain high concentrations of the element aluminum. Beta amyloid is a primary protein that collects in these damaged areas. It appears to be derived from a larger protein called amyloid precursor protein (APP). These precursor proteins are abnormal proteins that become deposited in healthy tissues and interfere with normal functioning. Scientists are now investigating drugs that may act to "mop up" APPs before they can collect, as well as substances that may someday be used to "replace" neurotransmitters that have become depleted in the brains of persons with Alzheimer's disease.

Today nearly one in six elderly persons has Alzheimer's disease. With America's over-65 population increasing, scientists are stepping up their efforts to counteract the disease. So far, however, most of these efforts have shown only limited promise.

Moreover, Alzheimer's disease is only one of approximately 50 medical problems that affect memory and intellect—either or both of which are usually at risk whenever injury or illness strikes the brain. Indeed, memory problems are often a sign that someone has suffered brain damage. Brain tumors, head injuries, infections in the brain, certain vitamin deficiencies, oxygen deprivation, diabetes, epilepsy, and severe depression can all disrupt memory.

AMNESIA

Movies and TV programs show it all the time: a character sustains a head injury and awakens without any memory of his or her identity or former life. A number of complications arise until the character is somehow once again hit on the head, causing a return of memory. To many people, this scenario represents *amnesia*.

True, a blow to the head can harm the brain and cause widespread memory loss, but the term amnesia does not refer only to this kind of memory impairment. Rather, it describes various disorders of memory that have any number of causes. Reactions to alcohol and drugs, for example, and even emotional trauma can trigger amnesia as readily as can an illness or injury. And the accompanying memory loss is usually different from that of the television scenario.

Although injury to various parts of the brain may affect different aspects of memory, there seem to be two general types of amnesia. In the first type, often referred to as retrograde amnesia, people forget their past, although usually only in part. Thus, someone who has a serious automobile accident may forget the five years before the accident but still recall events from his or her childhood.

The second form of amnesia, referred to as anterograde amnesia, results from the inability to create new memories and so, essentially, to learn. The two types of amnesia often accompany one another and involve a loss of memory for events, people, or facts, rather than for language. Short-term memory is also rarely affected by either form of amnesia.

A severe case of amnesia, involving both types of the condition and documented by Dr. Brenda Milner at McGill University, affected H.M., a 27-year-old epilepsy patient of average intelligence. In 1953, doctors removed most of H.M.'s hippocampus and amygdala, as well as parts of his cerebral cortex, in an attempt to relieve him of his epileptic seizures. Tragically, the surgery destroyed much of his ability to remember and learn.

Today, no matter how many times H.M. meets someone, he cannot remember that person. He reads the same magazine repeatedly without getting bored, because he forgets it after each reading. And whenever he is reminded that his favorite uncle is dead, he experiences new grief. He has told his doctors that for him, "Every moment is like waking from a dream."

H.M. has also forgotten the several years just before his surgery, although he recalls his childhood and has been able to learn new motor skills, including tennis and puzzle solving. The ability to learn some new skills, but not to recall this learning experience, indicates that the hippocampus—the part of H.M.'s brain that was removed—is responsible for consolidating information after it has been coded. Needless to say, the surgical operation done to cure his epilepsy is no longer used.

Despite their disability, most persons with amnesia can learn new motor skills and remember old ones—although they may not recall the process of learning them. This is clearly demonstrated by the case of an amnesiac who played golf on each of several consecutive days. Although he could not remember from one day to the next that he had played on the previous day, he steadily improved his game. Such cases support the idea that different types of memory—for instance, procedural memory versus factual memory—are governed by brain structures that operate independently.

Head Injuries

An estimated 2 million or more head injuries occur yearly in the United States. Reportedly, half of these injuries are automobile related, while a third result from falls or sports activities. Such injuries often impair memory to some degree, although not as severely as television and movies might suggest. Persons who suffer amnesia as the result of a mild or moderate head injury often recover their memory with the passage of time—although not by receiving another blow on the head.

Boxers with the so-called *punch-drunk syndrome*—a condition caused by brain damage from repeated blows to the head—are victims of a special kind of head injury; neurons in their brains may show similarities to those of Alzheimer's disease patients, and they experience both physical and mental problems, including memory loss.

An estimated 10% to 15% of professional boxers may be permanently punch-drunk. The renowned world heavyweight boxing

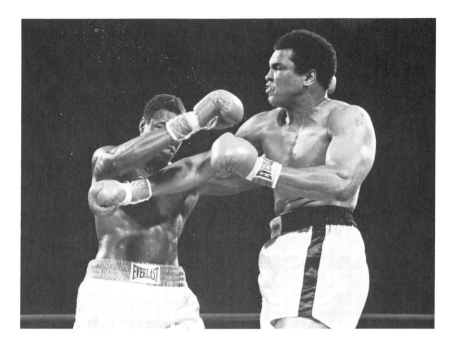

Boxer Larry Holmes (left) connects with Muhammad Ali during a fight for the heavyweight championship in Las Vegas, Nevada, in 1980. Holmes retained his title after Ali failed to answer the bell for the 11th round. The punch-drunk syndrome, a condition that produces memory loss and other mental as well as physical impairment, now affects Ali as it has many other boxers after long prizefighting careers.

champion Muhammad Ali is now suffering such effects from his boxing career. Cases such as Ali's have led some medical authorities to call for strict rules requiring boxers to wear helmets when they box.

Drug Abuse

Ethyl alcohol and other drugs have a variety of effects on the brain. They can at least temporarily affect memory and, with heavy use, can interfere with memory and learning for much longer periods. In extreme cases, years of heavy alcohol consumption, accompanied by poor eating habits, cause the disease known as *Korsakoff's psychosis*. Although Korsakoff's psychosis is often accompanied by both of the two types of amnesia, it particularly seems to affect the ability to transfer new information from short- to long-term memory. When examining the brains of patients with this psychosis, researchers have found extensive damage to the thalamus, a brain area involved in memory coding and transfer.

The Boston neurologist Oliver Sacks described two patients with Korsakoff's psychosis in his book *The Man Who Mistook His Wife for a Hat*, describing several cases of patients with neurologic disorders affecting memory and cognition. One of these patients, a 60-year-old man, believed in 1986 that World War II had just ended and that he himself was 20 and just out of the navy. Another man believed that he was still serving his customers in a grocery store that he had once owned, although he had been hospitalized for many years. Neither man could recall new faces or facts for more than a few moments.

Scientists still do not fully understand the mechanism by which *ethanol,* the alcohol found in fermented or distilled liquors, interferes with short- or long-term memory. Some research indicates that ethanol activates numerous neurotransmitters in a complex series of interactions. Experiments with ethanol given to mice suggest that the inhibitory neurotransmitter called *gamma-aminobutyric acid (GABA)* is involved in the behavioral changes caused by drinking alcoholic

Although heavy drinkers may be highly convivial and sociable, the effects of alcohol may ultimately be highly destructive to their health. Victims of Korsakoff's psychosis suffer severe, debilitating memory loss.

beverages. GABA induces many of the common responses to ethanol, including sedation, reduction of anxiety, and motor incoordination.

In addition to their work with alcohol and drunkenness, scientists have also studied the effects of marijuana—another widely abused substance—on thought processes. Marijuana contains *delta 9-tetra-hydrocannabinol (THC)*, a chemical substance whose molecules fit into some of the specialized structures known as receptors. These receptors exist on the cell membranes of neurons and are the sites where neurotransmitters and other substances act to exert their effects on neurons in the brain. Once activated by THC, these cells release natural substances within the brain that cause sedation, perceptual alterations, and euphoria. Like alcohol, marijuana causes intoxication by inducing numerous chemical processes within the brain.

Research confirms that both STM and learning ability are impaired for several hours after marijuana use. Someone who has just smoked marijuana may, for example, begin a sentence and forget what he or she was saying. Research has given conflicting information about the effects of marijuana on long-term memory. Marijuana does produce brain cell damage in monkeys, but this effect has not been proven in humans.

Benzodiazepines

Another type of drug, often prescribed by doctors to reduce anxiety or help a patient sleep, can also interfere with memory. These drugs are the benzodiazepines, which include diazepam (Valium) and, more recently, Halcion. Besides causing amnesia, these drugs can produce stupor and even coma.

Stroke

Another cause of memory loss is *stroke*, a condition that results from the bursting of a blood vessel in the brain or the blockage of a blood vessel in the brain by a blood clot, stopping the vital supply of blood and oxygen to the brain. Strokes are the third leading cause of death in the United States, but they are not always fatal. A series of small strokes, caused by gradual clogging of the blood vessels that feed the brain, may produce a mental state similar to that in Alzheimer's disease.

In more than a million Americans, strokes cause *aphasia*, or loss of the ability to use language. This often results from damage to the brain's left hemisphere. If the damage occurs in the region of the frontal lobe called Broca's area, it produces motor aphasia, which involves difficulties in speaking and writing. Sensory aphasia—characterized by an incapacity to understand speech or produce meaningful phrases in the order intended—comes from damage to Wernicke's area, a region in the posterior temporal lobe. Damage to other brain areas may produce *alexia*, an inability to read, and *agraphia*, an inability to write.

Many people survive strokes, although their memories may be permanently affected. However, young children who suffer harm to the left hemisphere often overcome language-related problems without any sign of lasting damage. Scientists explain this recovery by observing that early in development, the right hemisphere can still com-

The brain's left hemisphere, in which are located the centers that govern language production and comprehension. Broca's area, in the frontal lobe, contains the motor areas for speech and controls the tongue, lips, and vocal cords. Although located in the left hemisphere in right-handed persons, Broca's area is found in the right hemisphere in those who are left-handed.

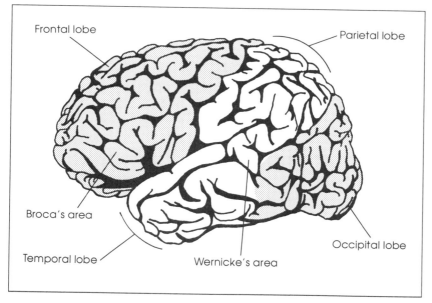

91

pensate for functions normally performed by the left hemisphere. Unfortunately, this ability diminishes with age, so that older people who lose the ability to speak, read, or otherwise use language as the result of a stroke seldom recover from the damage.

EXTRAORDINARY MEMORY

Most people believe that memory disorders refer only to the loss of memory. Although the vast majority of such disorders do involve memory loss, an extraordinarily good memory can also cause problems. One such case, reported in the 1960s by well-known Russian psychologist Alexander Luria, showed that remembering too much can be as troublesome as remembering too little.

An individual identified only as S., who was a 30-year-old newspaper reporter, did not forget anything. When asked to memorize a long list of words or numbers, S. always recalled it perfectly, within a matter of seconds or minutes—even when it included more than 100 items. S. also remembered such lists more than 15 years after seeing them, no matter how meaningless their contents. When recalling written lists, S. would see a copy of the list in his mind and read from it as if it were actually in front of him. He could therefore recite a list forward or backward.

When he heard lists of words instead of seeing them, S. would remember them by associating visual images with each word and then arranging the images in order along an imaginary street. As in the ancient Greek memory houses, S. would take a mental walk down the imaginary street to recite the list.

Eventually, S. left his newspaper job and supported himself as a professional *mnemonist* (a person with exceptional memory) by performing memory feats for audiences. However, his inability to forget the thousands of lists and other insignificant information he carried in his head became a nightmare. He tried to write down on paper everything that he wanted to forget and then burn the paper, but this did not get rid of the unwanted information. Finally, he discovered that he could put information on a mental blackboard and then imagine erasing it. In this way he was able to free himself of excess material.

LEARNING DISORDERS

A *learning disorder* is a condition that interferes with the ability to use one or more basic skills such as reading or spelling, despite the presence of an average or even a high intelligence. Learning disorders have gained attention in the past 25 years as society has learned to recognize them.

Celebrities, such as the Hollywood actresses Cher and Whoopi Goldberg; Olympic athletes, such as diver Greg Louganis and decathlon champion Bruce Jenner; and successful people in other walks of life have admitted to being learning disabled. Historical research also suggests that Thomas Edison, inventor of the light bulb, and fairy-tale writer Hans Christian Andersen had learning disorders.

Some estimates suggest that from 10% to 15% of Americans—most of them male—are learning disabled. About 2 million of these people are between the ages of 6 and 21. Learning disorders are often diagnosed when a person's abilities are generally at the proper level for the person's age but deficient in the case of a specific skill. For instance, Richard Sullivan, codirector of the Center for Learning Disorders in New York City, recalls a 15-year-old boy whose IQ of 135 put him in the category of highly intelligent but who could not remember the multiplication tables.

There are different types of learning disorders. *Dyslexia* refers to difficulty with reading. Dyslexic persons may not be able to make out

Dyslexia is a condition in which an individual is unable to interpret written language even though he or she has normal vision and intelligence. This child works on a computer program designed to help dyslexic persons learn to read.

the meaning of words or may see the letters reversed or the order of the words mixed up on a printed page. Other learning-disabled people may encounter problems with mathematics. In general, children with a learning disability make troublesome students because they have difficulty concentrating and are therefore restless and unable to sit still for long.

Learning disabilities remain a mysterious problem. In trying to explain them, experts often speak of "crossed wires" in the brain. Beyond that, their cause is not clear. According to Richard Sullivan, there are no cures for learning disorders, no way to uncross the wires. He explains that only long, hard work will compensate for the disability.

As more scientists, educators, and parents recognize learning disabilities early in youngsters' lives, they will be able to offer help sooner. Most schools provide programs that give learning-disabled children concentrated attention throughout the day or several times each day or per week. Parents also learn techniques for understanding their child's needs and helping him or her to learn at a comfortable pace.

In certain cases, doctors may prescribe medications that are meant to help a learning-disabled child to focus his or her attention by stimulating the central nervous system. However, like most medications, these often have side effects, including disrupted sleep and decreased appetite. And they do not completely correct the learning disability.

The human brain has taken billions of years to evolve. Its amazing ability to absorb and process vast amounts of information requires an immeasurable number of minute, exact, and instantaneous interactions. Every interaction occurs in an entirely new and unique way, depending on each individual's past lessons and present memories.

Science fiction stories suggest that computers may someday take over these functions for humans. Despite tremendous advances in computer technology in recent years, this scenario seems unlikely. But scientists hope that as they continue to study the inner workings of the mind, they will gain ground in improving the human ability to learn and to remember.

APPENDIX

APPENDIX:
FOR MORE INFORMATION

The following is a list of organizations that can provide information about learning and memory.

GENERAL INFORMATION

Alzheimer's Disease
Alzheimer's Association
919 North Michigan Avenue, Suite 1000
Chicago, IL 60611
(800) 272-3900

Alzheimer Society of Canada
1320 Yonge Street
Suite 201
Toronto, Ontario M4T 1X2
(416) 925-3552

National Institute on Aging
Information Office
9000 Rockville Pike
Building 31, Room 5C27
Bethesda, MD 20892
(301) 496-1752

Strokes

National Institute for Neurological Disorders and Strokes
Building 31, Room 8A16
Bethesda, MD 20892
(301) 496-5751

Learning Disabilities

American Association of University Affiliated Programs for Persons with Developmental Disabilities (AAUAP)
8630 Fenton Street, Suite 410
Silver Springs, MD 20910
(301) 588-8252

American Speech-Language-Hearing Association
10801 Rockville Pike
Rockville, MD 20852
In MD: (301) 897-8682
Outside MD: (800) 638-8255

Association for Children and Adults with Learning Disabilities
4156 Library Road
Pittsburgh, PA 15234
(412) 341-1515

Association of Learning Disabled Adults
P.O. Box 9722, Friendship Station
Washington, DC 20016
(301) 593-1035

Council For Learning Disabilities
P.O. Box 40303
Overland Park, KS 66204
(913) 492-3840

National Center for Learning
  Disabilities
99 Park Avenue, 6th Floor
New York, NY 10016
(212) 687-7211

The Orton Dyslexia Society
Chester Building, Suite 382
8600 LaSalle Road
Baltimore, MD 21204
(800) ABC-D123

Depression

American Mental Health Foundation
2 East 86th Street
New York, NY 10028

Canadian Mental Health Association
2160 Yonge Street
3rd Floor
Toronto, Ontario M4S 2Z3
(416) 484-7750

National Depressive and Manic Depressive Association
Box 3395
Chicago, IL 60654
(312) 993-0066

National Institute of Mental Health
Parklawn Building
5600 Fishers Lane
Rockville, MD 20857
(301)443-4513

Head Injuries

National Head Injury Foundation
P.O. Box 567
Framingham, MA 01710

FURTHER READING

Allport, Susan. *Explorers of the Black Box.* New York: Norton, 1986.

Blakemore, Colin. *Mechanics of the Mind.* London: Cambridge University Press, 1977.

Crowder, Robert G. *Principles of Learning and Memory.* Hillsdale, NJ: Lawrence Erlbaum Assocs., 1976.

Duggan, Nancy B. *Open House: A Visit to a Learning Disabilities Resource Room.* Danville, IL: Interstate Printers and Publishers, 1987.

Gallant, Roy A. *Memory: How It Works and How to Improve It.* New York: Four Winds Press, 1985.

Hooper, Judith, and Dick Teresi. *The Three-Pound Universe.* New York: Macmillan, 1986.

Loftus, Elizabeth. *Memory: Surprising New Insights Into How We Remember and Why We Forget.* Reading, MA: Addison-Wesley, 1980.

Sacks, Oliver. *The Man Who Mistook His Wife for a Hat and Other Clinical Tales.* New York: Summit Books, 1986.

GLOSSARY

acetylcholine a neurotransmitter that carries signals from one nerve cell to another

adrenaline a hormone released during stress that can either impair or enhance memory

age-associated memory impairment (AAMI) a natural degree of memory loss associated with aging

aggression behavior that is intended to inflict physical or psychological harm on others

agraphia inability to write, caused by brain damage

alexia inability to read, caused by brain damage

Alzheimer's disease a disease that usually strikes people over the age of 65 and results in permanent, severe memory loss

amnesia a memory disorder resulting from illness, injury, substance abuse, or emotional trauma; it can affect recall of the past or make learning impossible by preventing the formation of new memories

amygdala the part of the limbic system believed to be responsible for associating sensory memories and for linking memories with emotions

aphasia loss of the ability to use language, caused by injury to the brain's left hemisphere

Aplysia a genus of sea slug used in research on memory and learning

arteries the tubular channels that carry blood from the heart through the body; the hardening of the arteries that occurs with age can affect blood flow to the brain and impair memory

association the process by which a person mentally connects separate perceptions or ideas in a way that makes them meaningful

axon the long, narrow part of a nerve cell that carries messages for transmission to other cells

bovine cortex phosphatidylserine a naturally occurring substance found in cow brains that may help humans to restore their memories and ability to learn

cell assembly a cluster of neurons that was formerly believed to be the basis of memory retention

cerebellum the part of the brain responsible for learning repeated actions and retaining them in procedural memory

cerebral cortex the part of the brain that is the center of human learning, thinking, talking, and remembering

cerebral hemispheres the two halves of the forebrain, each of which contains structures responsible for specific functions

chunking a method of grouping information that enables short-term memory to store more information

circuits pathways between groups of neurons in the brain

classical conditioning a type of conditioning in which a reflexive response to a stimulus can be transferred to a second stimulus when the two stimuli are closely associated in time or place

cognitive learning a type of learning in which internal mental processes alter behavior

concept learning learning by classifying things according to their shared features

conceptual hierarchy a type of organizational system in which information in long-term memory is stored in large categories or sets

conditioned response a learned response made in reaction to a stimulus

conditioning the teaching of animals or humans to make mental associations

decay theory a theory suggesting that the passage of time weakens memory

declarative memory the ability to recall facts and events

deep structure the most fundamental meaning of words in a phrase; the intended meaning of a phrase that is stored in memory

delta-9-tetra-hydrocannabinol (THC) a substance found in marijuana that causes sedation, perceptual alterations, and euphoria

dendrite the branchlike part of a nerve cell that receives messages from other nerve cells

depression a mental condition that affects millions of Americans, characterized by a deep sense of sorrow and hopelessness

dyslexia a learning disorder characterized by difficulty in reading

elaborative rehearsal deliberate thought about information and its conscious association with already-known facts

episodic memory the ability to recall past events; the type of memory most affected by aging

ethanol the alcohol found in beer, wine, and distilled spirits

false memory inaccurate memory prompted by external suggestion or persuasion

flashbulb memories vivid, complete recollections of the surroundings in which a shocking experience occurred

forebrain the area of the cerebral cortex that is positioned behind the forehead and is divided into two halves called cerebral hemispheres

forgetting curve a mathematical graph that depicts how the passage of time affects memory recall

frontal lobes the paired regions of each cerebral hemisphere that are responsible for such uniquely human functions as self-awareness, initiative, and planning

gamma-aminobutyric acid (GABA) an inhibitory neurotransmitter responsible for refining and focusing the activity of the brain into meaningful patterns

glucose a naturally occurring sugar generated within the body that may improve memory

glutamate a neurotransmitter that activates communication between neurons in the hippocampus

habituation the establishment of a fixed pattern of behavior, or a fixed response to a particular stimulus

hippocampus the part of the limbic system believed to be responsible for the association and recall of spatial relationships

implicit memory the memory of motor skills

infantile amnesia a theory claiming that some early childhood memories are charged with primitive sexual feelings and are therefore blocked out of the conscious mind during adulthood

insight a type of cognitive learning that helps humans and some animals to solve problems

instinct an inborn, natural reflex that protects an organism

interference theory a theory stating that interruption of the thought process, rather than the passage of time, weakens memory

internal device a theoretical feature of the mind that some scientists believe enables small children to interpret adult speech, to perceive basic grammatical rules, and to form sentences

Korsakoff's psychosis a disease caused by continuous alcohol abuse and characterized by amnesia and the inability to learn

learned helplessness a condition in which animals or humans stop attempting to alter an unpleasant situation and subsequently become depressed

learned optimism the development of a thought system that can be used to combat despair or helplessness

learning a relatively permanent change in behavior, occurring because of experience or practice; an active process in which a usable skill or knowledge is gained

learning disorder a condition that causes difficulty in the acquisition of basic skills such as reading or spelling

limbic system a structure within the brain consisting of the hippocampus and amygdala; it plays an important role in transferring information from short-term memory to long-term memory storage

long-term memory the facility by which the brain stores a vast array of facts, impressions, and experiences

memory the process of retaining and recalling information that has been learned

memory trace the physical explanation for memory and learning

methods of loci a technique that enables older people to improve and strengthen their memory by linking items to be remembered with familiar places

microelectrode a research device that sends an electrical stimulus to cells and transmits the cells responses to a machine

mnemonist a person with exceptionally acute memory

motivation a reward or other stimulus that prompts an action

neurons nerve cells; the cells responsible for carrying information throughout the nervous system and brain

neuroscientist a specialist who studies the brain and nervous system

neurotransmitter a substance that transmits impulses through the synaptic space or gap between nerve cells

observational learning a type of learning in which the observation of behavior leads to memory and imitation of the observed behavior

olfactory nerve a structure within the head that detects and carries odors from the nose to the limbic system of the brain

operant conditioning a kind of conditioning that requires an action to accomplish a goal or gain a reward, whereby the association between the action and reward is strengthened by repetition

overlearning a process of repeated, conscious learning that aids in memory recall

phonological storage the remembering of number and letter lists according to their spoken sound rather than their written appearance

proactive interference a type of interference that occurs when old information is so deeply ingrained in memory that replacing it with new information becomes difficult

procedural memory the ability to learn skills and actions that can be automatically repeated without conscious thought; a type of memory based on repetitive practice

psyche the psychological characteristics of an individual

punch-drunk syndrome a group of physical and mental disabilities caused by brain damage from repeated blows to the head

punishment unpleasant consequences that follow unwanted behavior

puzzle boxes research experiment cages with doors that can be opened from inside by pulling on a string

reconstructive memory the way in which the retelling of a story is affected by previous or subsequent experience

reflex an automatic, natural, and uncontrollable response

reinforcement the process of rewarding actions to prompt associations

repression the inability to retrieve emotionally disturbing memories; the blocking out of unwanted or painful memories buried in the subconscious

retrieval the accessing of information stored in long-term memory

retroactive interference a type of interference occurring when newly acquired information interferes with the retrieval of previously stored information

reward a motivation for learning

rote rehearsal the continuous repetition of a fact in order to hold it in short-term memory for a longer than ordinary period so that is can enter into long-term memory

schema theory a theory claiming that expectations of events are based on past experience

selective breeding a process by which scientists interbreed members of an animal or plant species that share a specific trait, in order to observe the traits of the offspring

semantic memory the memory of vocabulary and facts

sensory memory a sensory impression that remains in the mind in its original form for one second or less

short-term memory a mechanism of memory that briefly holds incoming data before discarding it or transferring it to long-term memory

Skinner box a box used in research that contains a lever or similar mechanism that an animal learns to press or peck in order to get a food reward

stimulus something that affects the activity of a living organism

stroke a condition that results from interference with the supply of blood to the brain or a blood clot in a vessel

subconscious the part of the mind in which ideas, feelings, and memories exist below the level of normal awareness and which many scientists believe strongly influences a person's personality and behavior

subvocalization saying something to oneself in order to better prepare it for storage in long-term memory

surface structure the literal meaning of words in a phrase

synapses the spaces between nerve cells across which nerve signals are transmitted

thalamus the part of the brain that receives all incoming sensory information, except that of smell, before passing it on to the cortex and into long-term memory

vocalization saying something aloud in order to better prepare it for storage in long-term memory

INDEX

PICTURE CREDITS

Nancy Wartik is a freelance writer who lives in Brooklyn, New York. She is the author of *The French Canadians* in Chelsea House's THE PEOPLES OF NORTH AMERICA series, and is a contributing editor to *American Health* magazine. She has also written for *Ms.* magazine, the *Los Angeles Times Magazine*, *Publisher's Weekly*, and *Working Woman*.

LaVonne Carlson-Finnerty has been a staff writer for various magazines, including *16* and *Unique Homes*. Presently, she edits general interest books. In her free time, Carlson-Finnerty enjoys writing and directing plays.

Dale C. Garell, M.D., is medical director of California Children Services, Department of Health Services, County of Los Angeles. He is also associate dean for curriculum at the University of Southern California School of Medicine and clinical professor in the Department of Pediatrics & Family Medicine at the University of Southern California School of Medicine. From 1963 to 1974, he was medical director of the Division of Adolescent Medicine at Children's Hospital in Los Angeles. Dr. Garell has served as president of the Society for Adolescent Medicine, chairman of the youth committee of the American Academy of Pediatrics, and as a forum member of the White House Conference on Children (1970) and White House Conference on Youth (1971). He has also been a member of the editorial board of the *American Journal of Diseases of Children*.

C. Everett Koop, M.D., Sc.D., is former Surgeon General, deputy assistant secretary for health, and director of the Office of International Health of the U.S. Public Health Service. A pediatric surgeon with an international reputation, he was previously surgeon-in-chief of Children's Hospital of Philadelphia and professor of pediatric surgery and pediatrics at the University of Pennsylvania. Dr. Koop is the author of more than 175 articles and books on the practice of medicine. He has served as surgery editor of the *Journal of Clinical Pediatrics* and editor-in-chief of the *Journal of Pediatric Surgery*. Dr. Koop has received nine honorary degrees and numerous other awards, including the Denis Brown Gold Medal of the British Association of Paediatric Surgeons, the William E. Ladd Gold Medal of the American Academy of Pediatrics, and the Copernicus Medal of the Surgical Society of Poland. He is a chevalier of the French Legion of Honor and a member of the Royal College of Surgeons, London.